Microsoft Project 2016 - Creating a Project

Supports Project 2010 and 2013

In order to plan a project, information and resources must be gathered concerning various tasks involved to accomplish necessary tasks in order to generate an overall cost. **Microsoft Project** acts as a tool that assists in managing these projects. In this course, students will create a project by entering in the tasks, durations, and link tasks as well as create a project calendar. We will expand on the project by entering and assigning resources to a task and leveling the **Over-Allocated Resources**. Then we will manage the project by viewing the overall cost, setting the baseline, viewing the critical path, and updating completed tasks. Reports will display charts, text reports, and printouts of the overall project. At the end of the class, students will have the skills to create and manage exceptional project plans. The core features of **Projects 2010, 2013**, and **2016** are the same, however, the newer versions have added additional **Reporting** capabilities.

Table of Contents

Copyright and Release Information

Student Projects

Exercise Download

Exercises are posted on the website and can be downloaded to your computer.
Please do the following:

Open Internet Explorer/Edge: Or Google Chrome:

Type the web address: **elearnlogic.com/download/project2016-1.exe**

You might get several security warnings, but answer yes and run through each one. When you click
"**Unzip**," the files will be located in **C:\Data\Project2016-1** folder.

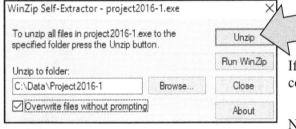

If there are any questions or problems, please contact Jeff Hutchinson at:

JeffHutch@elearnlogic.com

Note: For Mac users, download the file at:
elearnlogic.com/download/project2016-1.zip

About the Author

Jeff Hutchinson is a computer instructor teaching a variety of classes around the country. He has a BS
degree from BYU in Computer-Aided Engineering and has worked in the Information Technology field
supporting and maintaining computers for many years. He also previously owned a computer training and
consulting firm in San Francisco, California. After selling his business in 2001, he has continued to work
as an independent computer instructor/consultant around the country. Jeff Hutchinson lives in Utah and
also provides training for Utah Valley University Community Education system, offering valuable
computer skills for the general knowledge of students, career development, and career advancement.
Understanding the technology and the needs of students has been the basis for developing this material.
Jeff Hutchinson can be contacted at jeffhutch@elearnlogic.com or (801) 376-6687.

Design Strategy

This workbook is designed in conjunction with an Online-Instructor-Led course (for more information see: www.elearnlogic.com). Unlike other computer guides, students will not need to review lengthy procedures in order to understand a topic. All that is necessary are the brief statements and command paths located within the guide that demonstrate how a concept is used. There are many **Step-By-Step Practice Exercises** and more comprehensive **Student Projects** used to better understand a concept. Furthermore, students will find that this workbook guide is often used as a reference to help users understand concepts quickly. An index is also provided on the last page of the workbook to reference important topics as necessary. However, if more detail is needed for study, the Internet can be used to search for a concept. Also, if students' skills are weak due to lack of use, they can refresh their knowledge quickly by visually scanning the concept needed and then testing them out using the application.

Manual Organization

The following are special formatting conventions:
- **Numbered Sections** on the left are the **Concepts** covered.
- **Italic Text** is used to highlight commands that will perform the **Concept** or procedure in completing the practice exercises.
- **Practice Exercises** are a **Step-by-Step** approach to demonstrating the **Concept.**
- **Student Projects** are more comprehensive approaches to demonstrating the **Concept.**
- **Dark, Grayed-Out Sections** are optional/advanced **Concepts.**
- **Bolded** items are important **Concepts,** terminology, or commands used.
- **Tip** - These are additional ideas about the Concept.

Acknowledgment

This workbook/guide would not have been possible without the support of my wife, Doreen. Her writing skills and editing advice have been the greatest asset to polishing and clarifying its concepts. Thank you for your ongoing support.

Microsoft Project - Creating a Project

Chapter 1 - Views, Tables, And Formatting

We will first discuss various navigation techniques, different views available, table layouts, and also show the necessary steps needed to begin a new project.

Chapter Contents

Section 1 - Overview

Concept	Explanation / *Command String in italic.*
Practice Exercise 1	***File** tab→**Open**→ C:\Data\Project2016-1\House17.mpp.*
1.1 Views	There are many **Views** available. **Views** can be displayed using two methods. Method 1: ***Task Ribbon Tab→Gantt Chart drop-down.*** Method 2: ***View Ribbon Tab→Task Views and Resource Views Ribbon Group.***
Practice Exercise 2	The following are some common **Views** we will be using in this document: Commonly used **Views**: ***Tasks Ribbon Tab→Gantt Chart Dropdown:*** *Calendar, Net Diagram, Gantt Chart, Tracking Gantt, Timeline, Resource Sheet, Resource Usage, Resource Graph, and Team Planner.* More **Views**: ***Tasks Ribbon Tab→Gantt Chart Dropdown→More Views:*** *Resource Allocation, Detailed Gantt, and Gantt with Timeline.*
1.2 Table	The **Table** area is located on the left side of the interface. ***View Ribbon Tab→Data Group→Table dropdown.*** **Tip:** The **Entry Table** is the default **Table** for the Gantt Chart. Other useful **Tables** are **Cost**, **Summary**, and **Variance**.
Practice Exercise 3	Change the **Table** in the **Gantt Chart**: ***View Ribbon Tab→Data Group→Table drop-down→*** *Cost, Entry, Schedule, Tracking, Summary, and Variance.* **Tip:** When finished, be sure to switch back to the **Entry Table**.
1.3 Scroll To Task	This is one of the most useful commands in **Project**. It will allow you to navigate Bar Charts located on the right (if the Bar Chart is not visible). ***Select a task→Tasks Ribbon Tab→Scroll to Task.***
1.4 Zoom Slider	This is used to **Zoom** in and out and is located in the lower-left corner of the screen.

1.5 Gridlines	This will display Gridlines in the **Gantt Chart Bars** located on the right side of the interface. It is useful to line up **Bar Charts** with **Task Names**. In **Gantt Chart**: *Select a task→Format Ribbon Tab →▦ Gridlines →* *▦ Gridlines → Line to change: Gantt Rows→Type: Dash Line→Color: Gray.* 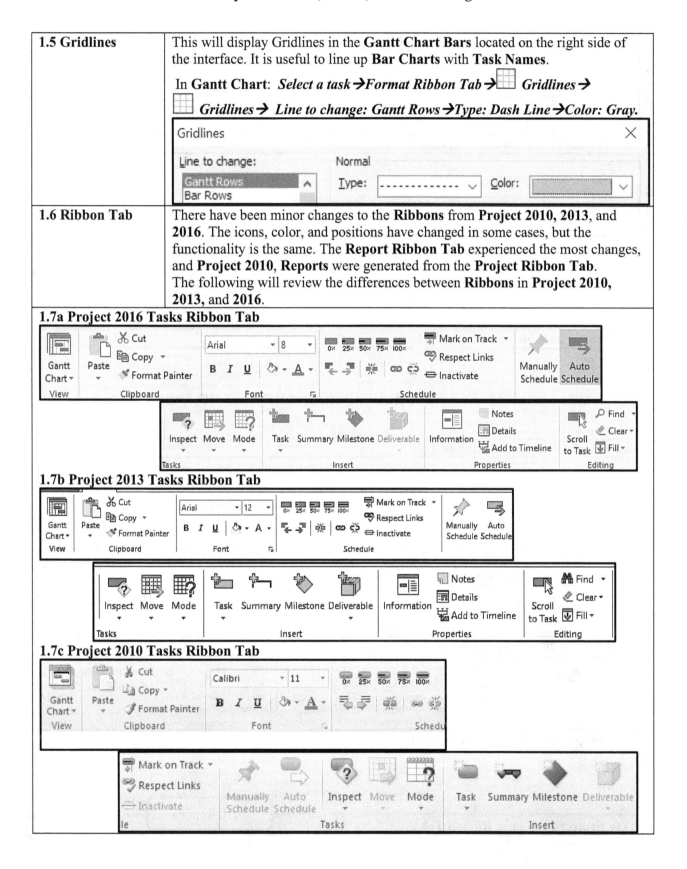
1.6 Ribbon Tab	There have been minor changes to the **Ribbons** from **Project 2010, 2013,** and **2016**. The icons, color, and positions have changed in some cases, but the functionality is the same. The **Report Ribbon Tab** experienced the most changes, and **Project 2010, Reports** were generated from the **Project Ribbon Tab**. The following will review the differences between **Ribbons** in **Project 2010, 2013,** and **2016**.

1.7a Project 2016 Tasks Ribbon Tab

1.7b Project 2013 Tasks Ribbon Tab

1.7c Project 2010 Tasks Ribbon Tab

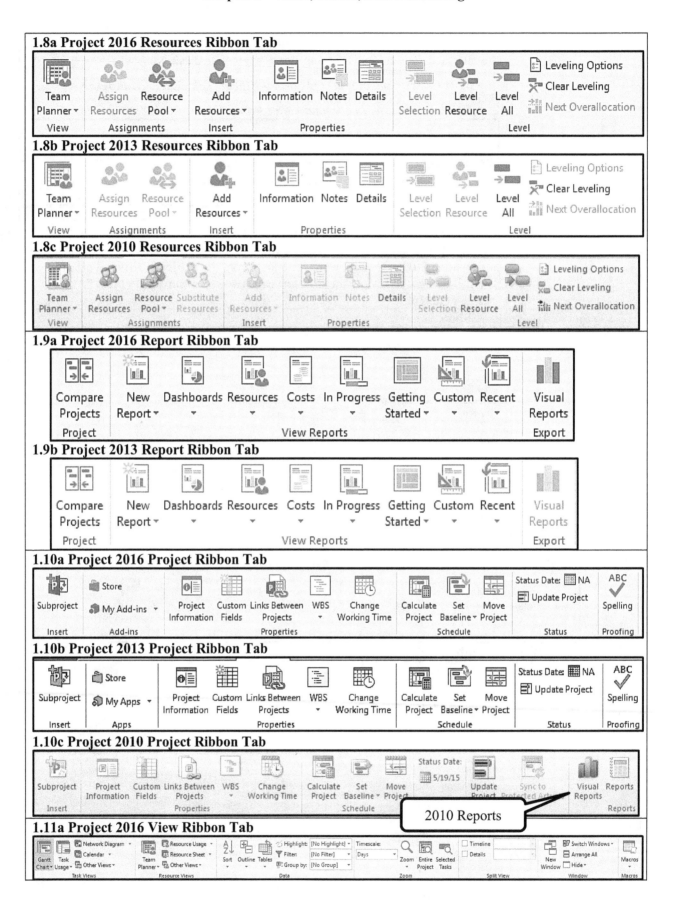

1.8a Project 2016 Resources Ribbon Tab

1.8b Project 2013 Resources Ribbon Tab

1.8c Project 2010 Resources Ribbon Tab

1.9a Project 2016 Report Ribbon Tab

1.9b Project 2013 Report Ribbon Tab

1.10a Project 2016 Project Ribbon Tab

1.10b Project 2013 Project Ribbon Tab

1.10c Project 2010 Project Ribbon Tab

2010 Reports

1.11a Project 2016 View Ribbon Tab

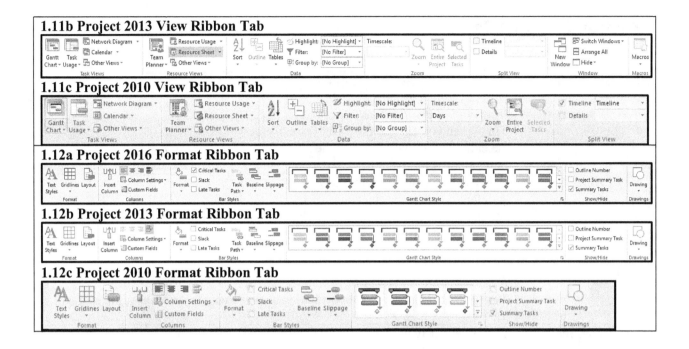

1.11b Project 2013 View Ribbon Tab

1.11c Project 2010 View Ribbon Tab

1.12a Project 2016 Format Ribbon Tab

1.12b Project 2013 Format Ribbon Tab

1.12c Project 2010 Format Ribbon Tab

Section 2 - Initial Setup Of A Project

The following items should be performed when starting a new project:

1.13 Start Date	This will set the **Start Date** of the project: ***Project Ribbon Tab→Project Information→Start Date.*** **Tip:** When you change the **Start Date**, the entire Project will move to the new **Start Date**.
1.14 Properties	This will define the project title. A default name is the file name and the file name may be different than the project title. ***File Tab→Info→Project Information→Advanced Properties→Title.*** **Tip:** When you generate a report or display the **Project Summary**, the title will be used.
1.15 Calendar	This is primarily used for holidays that may span the planned project. When the task's **Start** and **Finish** dates cross over a holiday, it will skip that day and extend the task. ***Project Ribbon Tab→Change Working Time.*** 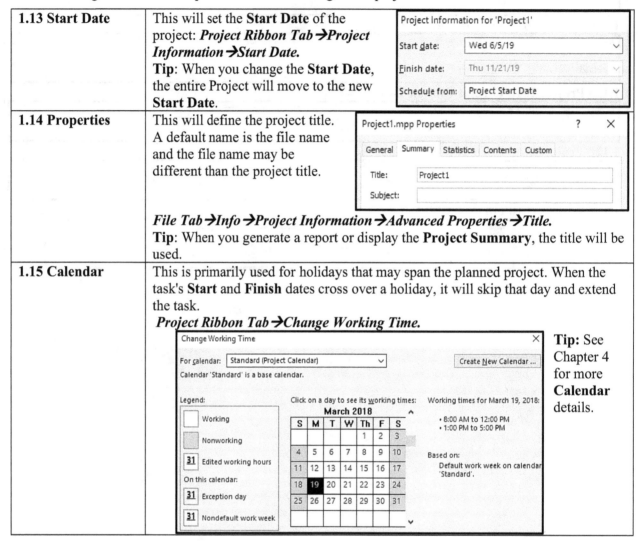

Student Project A - Initial Setup Of A Project

1. Create a new blank project: ***File Tab→New→Blank Project.***
2. Set the start date for a new project: ***Project Ribbon Tab→Project Information→Start Date:*** *(Enter one month or when your project will begin).*
3. Define the Project Name: ***File Tab→Info→Project Information→Advanced Properties:*** *Title: (Enter the name of the project).*
4. Set up the Calendar: ***Project Ribbon Tab→Change Working Time→*** *(Enter the holidays over the next year).*

Chapter 2 - Tasks, Durations, and Organization

In this chapter, we will enter the tasks, durations, and organize the summary tasks.

Concept	Explanation / *Command String in italic.*
Practice Exercise 4	*File Tab→New→Blank Project.*
2.1 Task Names	The **Task Name** must be descriptive and all names must be different. The order of the **Task Names** (from top to bottom) should be successive from start to finish. **Tip**: The **Task Name** is called **Name** in the **Project** database.
2.2 Manually Schedule	The **Manually Schedule** is used in the beginning to estimate tasks and durations. The actual scheduled dates will not be available at this time. In the **Manually Scheduled** mode, the duration field can be entered as a text description or a numeric value. The actual duration value must be entered when you convert the field to **Auto-Schedule**. *Task Ribbon Tab→Manually Schedule.*
Practice Exercise 5	Type in the following tasks:

Task Mode ▾	Task Name ▾	Duration ▾	S	M	T	W	T	F	S	S	M
⭐?	Task 1	*One day before inspection*									
⭐?	Task 2	5 days									
⭐?	Task 3	*Check with finance*									

Concept	Explanation / *Command String in italic.*
2.3 Duration Value	A **Duration** is the amount of work performed. **Durations** can be abbreviated to enter it faster. ⟶ **Tip: 1mo** represents months and **1m** represents 1 minute. **1mo** uses an average of 20 working days, which is the average of one month over several months. **1d=1Day** **1w=1Week** **1mo=1Month** **1h=1Hour** **1m=1Minute** **1s=Second**
2.4 Auto-Schedule	When the **Duration Column** is all listed as actual numeric duration values (example 2d), then select all the tasks and click the **Auto-Schedule**. This will schedule the actual **Start** and **Finish Dates** on the **Gantt Chart**. **Tip**: When new tasks are added, don't forget to set it to **Auto-Schedule**. (See 2.8 to set the default to **Auto-Schedule**). *Task Ribbon Tab→Auto-Schedule.*
Practice Exercise 6	***Continue from the previous Blank Project.*** **1. *Change the following durations to the following:***

Task Mode ▾	Task Name ▾	Duration ▾	Start ▾	Finish ▾	T	F	S	S	M	T	W	T	F
⭐?	Task 1	2 days											
⭐?	Task 2	5 days											
⭐?	Task 3	1 wk											

2. Select the 3 tasks →Task Ribbon Tab →Auto-Schedule.

Task Mode ▾	Task Name ▾	Duration ▾	Start ▾	Finish ▾	T	F	S	S	M	T	W	T	F
➡	Task 1	2 days	Fri 1/1/16	Mon 1/4/16									
➡	Task 2	5 days	Fri 1/1/16	Thu 1/7/16									
➡	Task 3	1 wk	Fri 1/1/16	Thu 1/7/16									

2.5 Task Mode	**Task Mode** is an indicator showing the status of the **Manually/Auto-Schedule**. ⟨⟩ – This needs more information in order to be ready to set to **Auto-Schedule** mode. ⟨⟩ - This means the task has been set to **Auto-Schedule** mode. **Tip:** If this column is not displayed: *Right-Click on any column label→ ⟨⟩ Insert Column→Task Mode.*
2.6 Milestone	**Milestones** are generally 0 length duration and are a single instant in time. A **Milestone** is usually at the end of a group of tasks concluding in a group of tasks. Enter a 0-day duration (od) in the **Duration Column** to create a **Milestone**. This places a small diamond on the schedule similar to: ◆ 6/7 . **Tip: Milestones** should be linked to the predecessor task.
Practice Exercise 7 *Milestone*	*Continue from the previous Blank Project.* 1. *Enter a Milestone and name it Task 4.* | Task 4 | 0 days | ◆ 6/7 | 2. *Select the Task4→Task Ribbon Tab→Auto-Schedule.* 	Task Mode	Task Name	Duration						Jun 9, '19			
			T	W	T	F	S	S	M	T	W
⟨⟩	Task 1	2 days	▬▬ 0%								
⟨⟩	Task 2	5 days								▬▬▬ 0%	
⟨⟩	Task 3	1 wk								▬▬▬ 0%	
⟨⟩	Task 4	0 days	◆ 6/5									
2.7 Reoccurring Task	Some tasks are **Reoccurring** such as "review meetings", or "team meetings." Oftentimes, these are scheduled separately and are not reflected in the project plan. *Task Ribbon Tab→Task Dropdown→Reoccurring button.*
Practice Exercise 8 *Reoccurring Task*	*Continue from the previous Blank Project.* 1. *Click on a blank task just under Task4.* *Task Ribbon Tab→Task Dropdown→Reoccurring button.* **Recurring Task Information** Task Name: Meeting Duration: 1h **Recurrence pattern** ○ Daily Recur every 1 week(s) on: ◉ Weekly ○ Monthly ☐ Sunday ☑ Monday ☐ Tuesday ☐ Wednesday ○ Yearly ☐ Thursday ☐ Friday ☐ Saturday **Range of recurrence** Start: Wed 6/5/19 ◉ End after: 3 occurrences ○ End by: Mon 6/24/19 3. The results will look similar to the following: | ⓘ	Task Name	Duration	Jun 5, '16							Jun 12, '16							Jun 19, '16	
			S	M	T	W	T	F	S	S	M	T	W	T	F	S	S	M
↻	⊿ Meeting	10.13 days	▪							▪							▪
⊞	Meeting 1	1 hr	▪															
⊞	Meeting 2	1 hr								▪								
⊞	Meeting 3	1 hr															▪	

2.8 Outline /Summary	This will organize tasks into groups or summarize the group of tasks that have a common purpose. A **Summary Group** will have the tasks indented. *Select a group of related tasks→Task Ribbon Tab→Summary.* **Tip:** Another way to create a summary is to manually insert the summary name, select the desired tasks, then choose *Task Ribbon Tab→Summary Button* `⌐¬ Summary`.
Practice Exercise 9 Outline	This will select tasks 2 and 3 and Indent where indicated. *Select tasks 2 and 3→Task Ribbon Tab→Summary button.* *Enter the name: MySummary.* Task Name	Duration	(Gantt chart) ▲ Task 1	5 days Task 2	5 days Task 3	1 wk Task 4	0 days	◆ 6/5
2.9 Move Task	Select the number in front of the task to **Move** it. 1. *Click the line number in front of the task→Let go of the mouse button→ Select it again and move it to the desired location.* 2. *Select task→Task2→(Move it under Task4).* Line Number (label) ① Task Name	Duration	Mar 25, '18 1	▲ Task 1	5 days 2	Task 2	5 days 3	Task 3	1 wk 4	Task 4	0 days	◆ 3/23
2.10 Outline Numbering	This will display the **WBS (Work Breakdown Structure)** in front of each task name and summary task. *Format Ribbon Tab→ ☑ Outline Numbering.* Task Name	Duration ▲ 1 Task 1	5 days 1.1 Task 3	1 wk 2 Task 4	0 days 3 Task 2	5 days ▲ 4 Meeting	10.13 days 4.1 Meeting 1	1 hr 4.2 Meeting 2	1 hr 4.3 Meeting 3	1 hr
2.11 Inactivate Task **Project 2010** **Project 2013** **Project 2016**	A new feature has been added that **Inactivates** a task. If a task is no longer needed, it can be inactivated instead of deleted. However, if a task is deleted, the outline numbering system will be adjusted. This could cause confusion if the task numbers are being tracked. Also, after **Inactivation**, you will need to fix the links. *Task Ribbon Tab→Inactivate.* `⊟ Inactivate`

2.12 Project Summary	This will add a new Project task to the top of the entry table and provide a summary for the entire list. ***Format Ribbon Tab→ ☑ Project Summary.***	<table><tr><td>Task Name ▾</td><td>Duration ▾</td></tr><tr><td>▲ **Project1**</td><td>**122 days?**</td></tr><tr><td>▲ **1 Task 1**</td><td>**5 days**</td></tr><tr><td>1.1 Task 3</td><td>1 wk</td></tr><tr><td>2 Task 4</td><td>0 days</td></tr><tr><td>3 Task 2</td><td>5 days</td></tr><tr><td>▲ **4 Meeting**</td><td>**10.13 days**</td></tr><tr><td>4.1 Meeting</td><td>1 hr</td></tr><tr><td>4.2 Meeting</td><td>1 hr</td></tr><tr><td>4.3 Meeting</td><td>1 hr</td></tr></table>
2.13 Estimate Task	When a task duration has a question mark, it indicates that the task is an **Estimate**. This can be used if the duration is in question or needs to be verified. It can be cleared by typing in the new duration without the question mark or turning off the **Estimation** check box. ***Double-Click on the task→Task Information→General tab→ ☑ Estimated***	
2.14 Delete A Task	To **Delete** a task: ***Select the desired task→Press the Delete Key or Right-Click on the row and choose Delete Task.***	
2.15 Undo/Redo	To **Undo** a task, press the ***Ctrl Z Key or press the*** 🔄 ***button in the upper left corner of the screen.*** To **Redo** a task, use the quick access toolbar located in the upper left corner of the screen ↪	
2.16 Insert Task	To **Insert** a new task: ***Select a task→Press the Insert Key.*** Or in each group: ***Right-Click on the task→Choose Insert task.***	
2.17 Summary Hide	This will turn off or **Hide** all summary tasks located within each group. ***Format Ribbon Tab→ ☑ Summary tasks.***	<table><tr><td>Task Name ▾</td><td>Duration ▾</td></tr><tr><td>1.1 Task 3</td><td>1 wk</td></tr><tr><td>2 Task 4</td><td>0 days</td></tr><tr><td>3 Task 2</td><td>5 days</td></tr><tr><td>4.1 Meeting</td><td>1 hr</td></tr></table>
2.18 Placeholder	A **Placeholder** task is anticipated for the future. It could be an unknown task or something that has not been yet defined. Some Projects Managers use this to establish a constant **WBS** outline numbering system.	
2.19 Default Auto Schedule	After you create a project plan, you might want to set the **Auto-Schedule** to be the default value for all new tasks. ***File Tab→Options→Schedule→New Tasks Created.*** | New tasks created:	Auto Scheduled ▾
---|---| **Tip:** This is useful because as you insert new tasks using the default of **Manually Schedule,** it will not schedule the dates or move the bar to the proper location. The **Manually Schedule** will look like the following: | Task Mode ▾	Task Name ▾	Duration ▾	S	M	T	W	T	F	S	S	M
---	---	---	---	---	---	---	---	---	---	---	---
✰?	Task 1	2 days									
✰?	Task 2	1 wk									
✰?	Task 3	3 days										

	The **Auto-Schedule** will look like the following:
		Task Mode ▾	Task Name ▾	Duration ▾	S	M	T	W	T	F	S	S	M
---	---	---	---	---	---	---	---	---	---	---	---	---	---
	⇨	Task 1	2 days	T								
	⇨	Task 2	1 wk	T								
	⇨	Task 3	3 days	T								
2.20 Team Planner	This allows you to see all unassigned tasks. *View Ribbon Tab→Team Planner.*
2.21 Entry Bar	The **Entry Bar** is similar to the **Excel** formula bar. *File Tab→Options→Display→ ☑ Entry Bar.* ✗ ✓ Task 1 Show these elements: ☑ Entry bar

Student Project B - Tasks, Duration And Organization
Open Blank Project: *File Tab→New→Blank project.*
Set the start date: *Project Ribbon Tab→Project Information→Start Date: 1/1/2019.*
Set up the Calendar: *Project Ribbon Tab→Change Working Time→add 4ᵗʰ of July and Labor Day.*

Enter tasks and durations
1. Conduct Site Survey
2. Develop Blueprints   Check with the designer.
3. Draft Proposal   3d
4. Request Bids   1w
5. Get Bids   1w
6. Build Foundation
7. Dig Foundation   3d
8. Pour Foundation   3d

Make the following changes to the tasks:
1. Change **Develop Blueprints** to **Develop Plan.**   **2w**
2. Change the duration of the **Draft Proposal** to **1w.**
3. Change the name of **Get Bids** to **Obtain Bids.**
4. Delete task: Delete the **Request Bid** task.
5. Undo: *Undo* the previous task or *Ctrl Z.*
6. Change the duration of **Request Bids** to **2d.**
7. Change Duration of **Conduct Site Survey** to **3d.**
8. Add a note to **Conduct Site Survey** of "**Return survey to the designer.**"

Add the following tasks:
9. Insert (**Insert Key**) above Build Foundation: Select Subcontractors.   3d
10. Insert (**Insert Key**) a Milestone above **Build Foundation: Complete Planning Phase. 0d**
11. Select all tasks and change to **Auto-Schedule.**

Recurring Task
12. Add a Reoccurring meeting: Select a blank task→*Task Ribbon Tab→ Insert ribbon group→Task Dropdown button→Recurring Task*
    Task Name: **Status Meeting,** ◉ Weekly, ◉ Monday, Duration: 1h
13. Change Reoccurring Task: *Double click on the reoccurring task→ Change meeting to* ◉ *Friday*

Outline Tasks
14. Indent **Dig Foundation** and **Pour Foundation** and insert under **Build Foundation.**

Show/Hide options:
15. *Format Ribbon Tab→Show/hide ribbon group → ☑ Outline Number.*
16. *Format Ribbon Tab→Show/hide ribbon group → ☑ Project Summary task.*

The Final Result will look similar to the following:

		Task Name	Duration	Timeline (4–18)
0		◢ Project3	10 days	
1		1 Conduct Site Survey	3 days	
2		2 Develop Plans	2 wks	
3		3 Draft Proposal	1 wk	
4		4 Request Bids	2 days	
5		5 Obtain Permits	1 wk	
6		6 Obtain Bids	1 wk	
7		7 Select Subcontractors	3 days	
8		8 Complete Planning Phase	0 days	◆ 6/5
9		◢ 9 Build Structure	3 days	
10		◢ 9.1 Build Foundation	3 days	
11		9.1.1 Dig Foundation	3 days	
12		9.1.2 Pour Foundation	3 days	
13	⟳	◢ 10 Status Meeting	5.13 days	

Chapter 3 - Linking

In this chapter, students will learn how to interlink tasks together and build task relationships. This is probably the most important aspect of the **Project**. When tasks are all linked, the **Start** and **Finish Dates** will be defined.

Concept	Explanation / *Command String in italic.*
3.1 Task Relationships	This is how **Microsoft Project** defines the relationship between tasks. **Predecessor** - This is the task pointing backward to the previous task. **Successor** - This is looking forward towards the next tasks.
Practice Exercise 10	1. *File Tab→New→Blank Project.* 2. *Create 10 tasks named Task 1 to Task 10.* 3. *Select all 10 tasks→Task Ribbon Tab→Auto-Schedule.* 4. *Select Task 1 and Task 2→Press the* 🔗 *Link Button.* 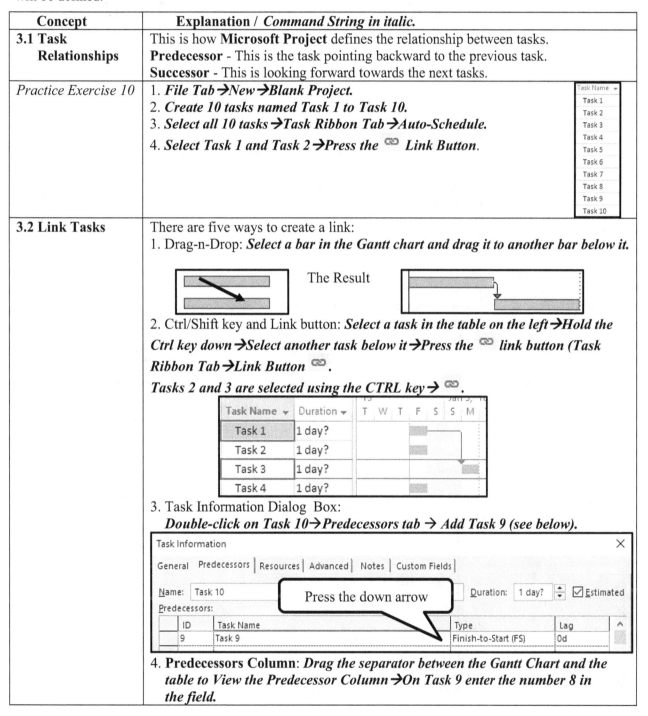
3.2 Link Tasks	There are five ways to create a link: 1. Drag-n-Drop: *Select a bar in the Gantt chart and drag it to another bar below it.*

The Result

2. Ctrl/Shift key and Link button: *Select a task in the table on the left→Hold the Ctrl key down→Select another task below it→Press the* 🔗 *link button (Task Ribbon Tab→Link Button* 🔗.

Tasks 2 and 3 are selected using the CTRL key→ 🔗.

Task Name	Duration	T	W	T	F	S	S	M
Task 1	1 day?							
Task 2	1 day?							
Task 3	1 day?							
Task 4	1 day?							

3. Task Information Dialog Box:
Double-click on Task 10→Predecessors tab → Add Task 9 (see below).

Task Information   ✕

General | Predecessors | Resources | Advanced | Notes | Custom Fields

Name: Task 10   Press the down arrow   Duration: 1 day? ☑ Estimated

Predecessors:

ID	Task Name	Type	Lag
9	Task 9	Finish-to-Start (FS)	0d

4. **Predecessors Column**: *Drag the separator between the Gantt Chart and the table to View the Predecessor Column→On Task 9 enter the number 8 in the field.*

Task Name	▼	Duration	▼	Start	▼	Finish	▼	Predecessors	▼
Task 8		1 day?		Tue 3/20/18		Tue 3/20/18			
Task 9		1 day?		Wed 3/21/18		Wed 3/21/18		8	
Task 10		1 day?		Thu 3/22/18		Thu 3/22/18		9	

5. This technique will link all tasks using the default of a **Start-To-Finish** relationship. You will need to ⛓**Unlink** (delete the links) between **Summary Tasks**. *Select all tasks→Press the* 🔗 *Link Button→Delete the links on the Summary tasks.*

3.3 Finish-To-Start (FS)	This is the most common relationship used in Project and is the default setting. The successor **Starts** when the predecessor **Finishes**. **Example 1:** Software is installed after a shipment is received. **Example 2:** Software development **Starts** after requirements **Finish**.
3.4 Start-To-Start (SS)	The successor **Starts** when the predecessor **Starts**. **Example 1:** The purchase of hardware and software occurs at the same time. **Example 2:** Developing software requirements and hiring engineers occur at the same time. **Tip:** They don't have to finish at the same time, but *must* start at the same time.
3.5 Finish-To-Finish (FF)	The successor **Finishes** when the predecessor **Finishes**. **Example 1:** Inspecting the electrical can't **Finish** until the wiring is **Finished**. **Tip:** They don't have to start at the same time but, *must* finish at the same time.
3.6 Start-To-Finish (SF)	The successor **Finishes** when the predecessor **Starts**. **Example 1:** Groundbreaking will occur when permits have been obtained. **Example 3:** You pay your bills when you receive your paycheck.
Practice Exercise 11 Start-To-Start	Continue from the previous Blank Project. ***Double click on a line connecting two bars→Change to a Start-To-Start.*** Task Dependency ✕ From: Task 9 To: Task 10 Type: Start-to-Start (SS) ⌄ Lag: 0d ⌄ Delete OK Cancel
3.7 Lead	**Lead** is used to accelerate a successor task. **Negative Lag** will allow tasks to overlap (-1d or -50%). **Example 1:** While you are finishing a task (such as documenting the results), the next task may begin.

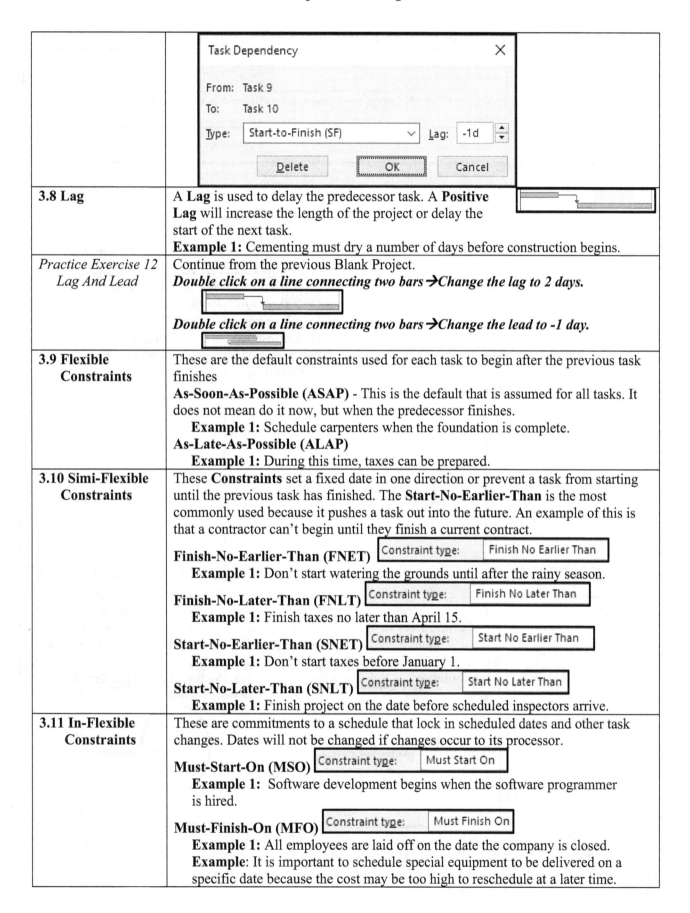

3.8 Lag	A **Lag** is used to delay the predecessor task. A **Positive Lag** will increase the length of the project or delay the start of the next task. **Example 1:** Cementing must dry a number of days before construction begins.
Practice Exercise 12 Lag And Lead	Continue from the previous Blank Project. ***Double click on a line connecting two bars →Change the lag to 2 days.*** ***Double click on a line connecting two bars →Change the lead to -1 day.***

3.9 Flexible Constraints	These are the default constraints used for each task to begin after the previous task finishes
	As-Soon-As-Possible (ASAP) - This is the default that is assumed for all tasks. It does not mean do it now, but when the predecessor finishes.
	    Example 1: Schedule carpenters when the foundation is complete.
	As-Late-As-Possible (ALAP)
	    Example 1: During this time, taxes can be prepared.

3.10 Simi-Flexible Constraints	These **Constraints** set a fixed date in one direction or prevent a task from starting until the previous task has finished. The **Start-No-Earlier-Than** is the most commonly used because it pushes a task out into the future. An example of this is that a contractor can't begin until they finish a current contract.
	
	Finish-No-Earlier-Than (FNET)
	    Example 1: Don't start watering the grounds until after the rainy season.
	
	Finish-No-Later-Than (FNLT)
	    Example 1: Finish taxes no later than April 15.
	
	Start-No-Earlier-Than (SNET)
	    Example 1: Don't start taxes before January 1.
	
	Start-No-Later-Than (SNLT)
	    Example 1: Finish project on the date before scheduled inspectors arrive.

3.11 In-Flexible Constraints	These are commitments to a schedule that lock in scheduled dates and other task changes. Dates will not be changed if changes occur to its processor.
	
	Must-Start-On (MSO)
	    Example 1: Software development begins when the software programmer is hired.
	
	Must-Finish-On (MFO)
	    Example 1: All employees are laid off on the date the company is closed.
	    Example: It is important to schedule special equipment to be delivered on a specific date because the cost may be too high to reschedule at a later time.

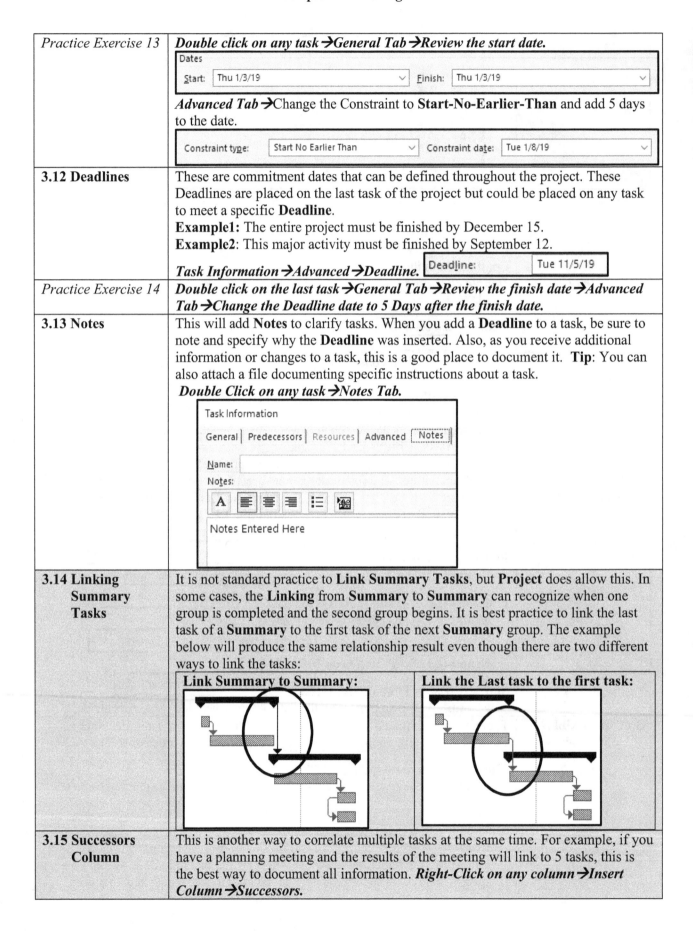

Practice Exercise 13	***Double click on any task→General Tab→Review the start date.*** Dates Start: Thu 1/3/19 Finish: Thu 1/3/19 ***Advanced Tab→***Change the Constraint to **Start-No-Earlier-Than** and add 5 days to the date. Constraint type: Start No Earlier Than Constraint date: Tue 1/8/19
3.12 Deadlines	These are commitment dates that can be defined throughout the project. These Deadlines are placed on the last task of the project but could be placed on any task to meet a specific **Deadline**. **Example1:** The entire project must be finished by December 15. **Example2**: This major activity must be finished by September 12. ***Task Information→Advanced→Deadline.*** Deadline: Tue 11/5/19
Practice Exercise 14	***Double click on the last task→General Tab→Review the finish date→Advanced Tab→Change the Deadline date to 5 Days after the finish date.***
3.13 Notes	This will add **Notes** to clarify tasks. When you add a **Deadline** to a task, be sure to note and specify why the **Deadline** was inserted. Also, as you receive additional information or changes to a task, this is a good place to document it. **Tip**: You can also attach a file documenting specific instructions about a task. ***Double Click on any task→Notes Tab.*** Task Information General | Predecessors | Resources | Advanced | [Notes] Name: Notes: A ≡ ≡ ≡ ☰ 🔢 Notes Entered Here
3.14 Linking Summary Tasks	It is not standard practice to **Link Summary Tasks**, but **Project** does allow this. In some cases, the **Linking** from **Summary** to **Summary** can recognize when one group is completed and the second group begins. It is best practice to link the last task of a **Summary** to the first task of the next **Summary** group. The example below will produce the same relationship result even though there are two different ways to link the tasks: **Link Summary to Summary:** | **Link the Last task to the first task:**
3.15 Successors Column	This is another way to correlate multiple tasks at the same time. For example, if you have a planning meeting and the results of the meeting will link to 5 tasks, this is the best way to document all information. ***Right-Click on any column→Insert Column→Successors.***

Student Project C – Link Practice
Open the following files and practice linking using the procedures above.
C:\Data\Project2016-1\Link Practice1.mpp
C:\Data\Project2016-1\Link Practice2.mpp
C:\Data\Project2016-1\Link Practice3.mpp

Student Project D - Linking
File tab→Open→C:\Data\Project2016-1\House3.mpp.
1. To Move a task: **Select Subcontractors** and move under **Obtain Bids.**
2. Insert a task above **Pour Foundation** and call it **Dig Foundation 3d.**
3. Indent or summarize the following:

⊿ Build Foundation	5 days
Dig Foundation	2 days
Pour Foundation	3 days
⊿ Construct Frame	12 days
Frame House	6 days
Frame Garage	3 days
Build Deck	3 days
⊿ Build Infrastructure	11 days
Initial Plumbing	7 days
Initial Electricity	2 wks
Security System	1 day
Drywall	4 days

4. Link all the tasks (using the 4 techniques discussed above) to the default relationship of **Finish-To-Start**. Don't forget to link the **Milestone** and skip over the **Summary** tasks.
5. **Lag:** Cement must dry 5 days before **Frame House** starts. Add a Lag of **5 days** between the **Pour Foundation** and **Frame House** tasks.

6. **Start-To-Start:** Change the relationship between the **Plumbing** and **Electricity** tasks to a **Start-To-Start** relationship.

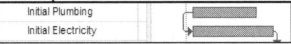

7. **Lead:** Add a Lead of **-2 days** between the **Obtain Bids** and **Select Subcontractors** tasks.

8. Change the relationship so the **Frame House** task drives both **Frame Garage** and **Build Deck** tasks.

9. Change the relationship so the **Develop Plan** task can start immediately. A double link must be added from **Develop Plans** and **Review Proposal** to **Request Bids**. Bids can't begin until both tasks are complete.

Conduct Site Survey	
Develop	
Draft Proposal	
Request Bids	
Request Permits	
Obtain Permits	

10. Add a **Deadline** to the Drywall task at the end of the project.

Security System	
Drywall	

11. Review the project plan and identify other changes such as **Start-To-Start**, **Finish-To-Finish**, **Lead**, **Lag**, **Constraint**, or **Deadlines**.

Student Project E - Linking Practice

File Tab→Open→C:\Data\Project2016-1\Rooms3.mpp

Complete, indent, and link the following by using the features in this chapter.

Note: In this project, we will be linking between summary tasks.

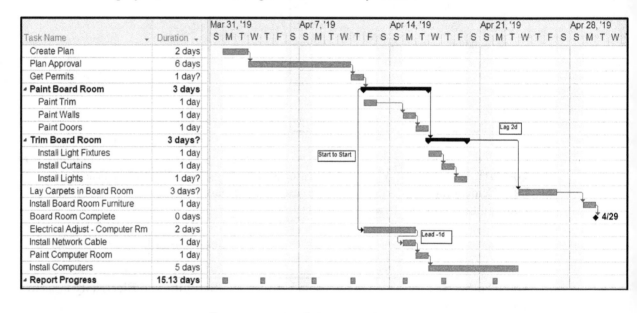

Task Name	Duration
Create Plan	2 days
Plan Approval	6 days
Get Permits	1 day?
⊿ **Paint Board Room**	**3 days**
Paint Trim	1 day
Paint Walls	1 day
Paint Doors	1 day
⊿ **Trim Board Room**	**3 days?**
Install Light Fixtures	1 day
Install Curtains	1 day
Install Lights	1 day?
Lay Carpets in Board Room	3 days?
Install Board Room Furniture	1 day
Board Room Complete	0 days
Electrical Adjust - Computer Rm	2 days
Install Network Cable	1 day
Paint Computer Room	1 day
Install Computers	5 days
⊿ **Report Progress**	**15.13 days**

Chapter 4 - Calendar

The main **Calendar** view located in (***Project Ribbon Tab→Change Working Time)***, is used to define new **Base Calendars** and modify **Resource Calendars**. You can create multiple **Base Calendars** used for a group of resources. These **Base Calendars** can display **Exceptions** (holidays) and **Work Week**, as well as abnormal work weeks or non-holidays.

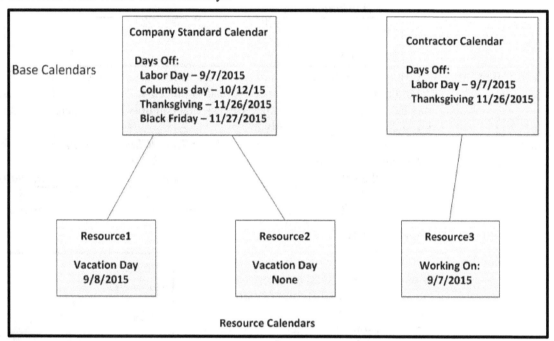

The above chart explains how the **Resource** and **Base Calendars** are related. **Resource1** will have a total of 5 days off, **Resource2** will have a total of 4 days off, and **Resource3** will have total of 1 day off. If an assigned task crosses over these off days, the task will be extended accordingly.

Chapter Contents

Section 1 - General Features

Concept	Explanation / *Command String in italic.*
Practice Exercise 18	*File Tab→New→Blank Project*
4.1 Standard Calendar	This is the default **Calendar**. If you only need one **Base Calendar**, then the **Standard Calendar** can be used. It contains three variations such as Standard (8-5, M-F), 24 hours, and Night Shift. For calendar: Standard (Project Calendar) ∨
4.2 Resource Calendar	A **Resource Calendar** is used to define vacation and time off. To create a **Resource Calendar** (vacation Calendar): ***View Ribbon Tab→Resource Sheet→(Add resource name)***. For calendar: Resource1 ∨ Base calendar: Standard ∨

	Tip: When you create a **Resource,** a **Resource Calendar** gets created automatically. Do not create the **Resource Calendar** the same way you create a **Base Calendar** because it will create a duplicate **Resource Calendar**.
Practice Exercise Resource Calendar	1. Create a Resource: *View Ribbon Tab→Resource Sheet→Resource Name: Resource1.* **Tip:** The Resource Calendar was created automatically**.** 2. Assign the resource to the **Standard Calendar**: *Project Ribbon Tab→ Change Working Time:* For calendar: Resource1 Base calendar: Standard
4.3 Task Calendar	A **Calendar** can be created and tied to a specific task. First, create a new Base Calendar then assign it to a specific task in the **Task Information Dialog Box**. This may be useful if you have a specific task that can only be conducted on a specific day such as on weekends only.
Practice Exercise Task Calendar	1. Create a Base Calendar: *Project Ribbon Tab→Change Working Time→ Create New Calendar→Calendar Name: Task Calendar.* 2. Assign the calendar to a task: *Double-Click on a task (Task Information)→ Advanced Tab→* Calendar: Task Calendar

Section 2 – Base Calendar

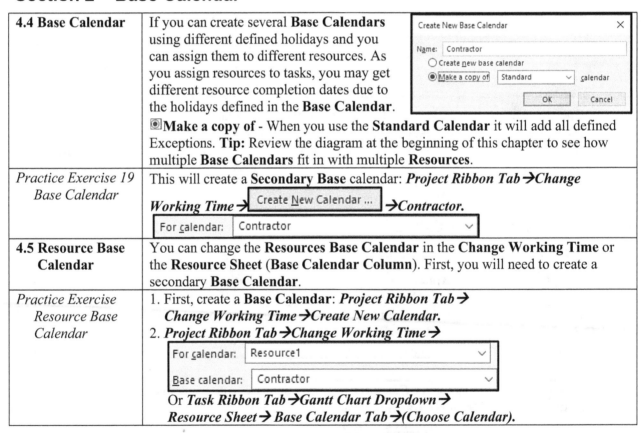

4.4 Base Calendar	If you can create several **Base Calendars** using different defined holidays and you can assign them to different resources. As you assign resources to tasks, you may get different resource completion dates due to the holidays defined in the **Base Calendar**.
	◉**Make a copy of** - When you use the **Standard Calendar** it will add all defined Exceptions. **Tip:** Review the diagram at the beginning of this chapter to see how multiple **Base Calendars** fit in with multiple **Resources**.
Practice Exercise 19 Base Calendar	This will create a **Secondary Base** calendar: *Project Ribbon Tab→Change Working Time→* Create New Calendar ... *→Contractor.* For calendar: Contractor
4.5 Resource Base Calendar	You can change the **Resources Base Calendar** in the **Change Working Time** or the **Resource Sheet (Base Calendar Column)**. First, you will need to create a secondary **Base Calendar**.
Practice Exercise Resource Base Calendar	1. First, create a **Base Calendar**: *Project Ribbon Tab→ Change Working Time→Create New Calendar.* 2. *Project Ribbon Tab→Change Working Time→* For calendar: Resource1 / Base calendar: Contractor Or *Task Ribbon Tab→Gantt Chart Dropdown→ Resource Sheet→ Base Calendar Tab→(Choose Calendar).*

Section 3 - Other Calendar Features

4.6 Calendar	The top part of a **Calendar** can be used to identify non-working days. ***Project Ribbon Tab→Change Working Time.***
	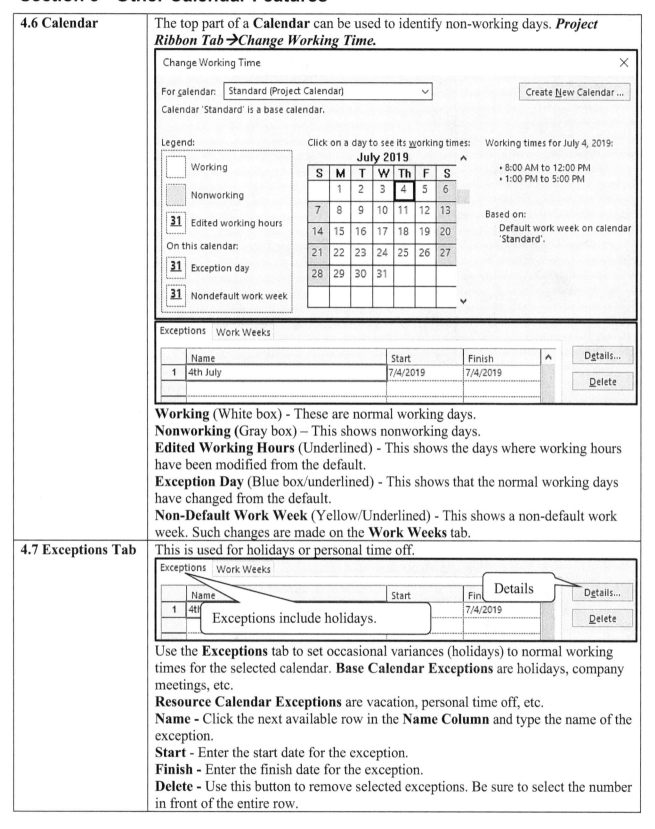
	Working (White box) - These are normal working days. **Nonworking** (Gray box) – This shows nonworking days. **Edited Working Hours** (Underlined) - This shows the days where working hours have been modified from the default. **Exception Day** (Blue box/underlined) - This shows that the normal working days have changed from the default. **Non-Default Work Week** (Yellow/Underlined) - This shows a non-default work week. Such changes are made on the **Work Weeks** tab.
4.7 Exceptions Tab	This is used for holidays or personal time off.
	Use the **Exceptions** tab to set occasional variances (holidays) to normal working times for the selected calendar. **Base Calendar Exceptions** are holidays, company meetings, etc. **Resource Calendar Exceptions** are vacation, personal time off, etc. **Name -** Click the next available row in the **Name Column** and type the name of the exception. **Start -** Enter the start date for the exception. **Finish -** Enter the finish date for the exception. **Delete -** Use this button to remove selected exceptions. Be sure to select the number in front of the entire row.

4.8 Exceptions Detail	**Details Button** - To adjust the day and time of the exception, first highlight the exception, then click the **Details** button. **Tip**: It is best to select the date in the calendar (top part of the **Dialog Box**) prior to typing in the name. 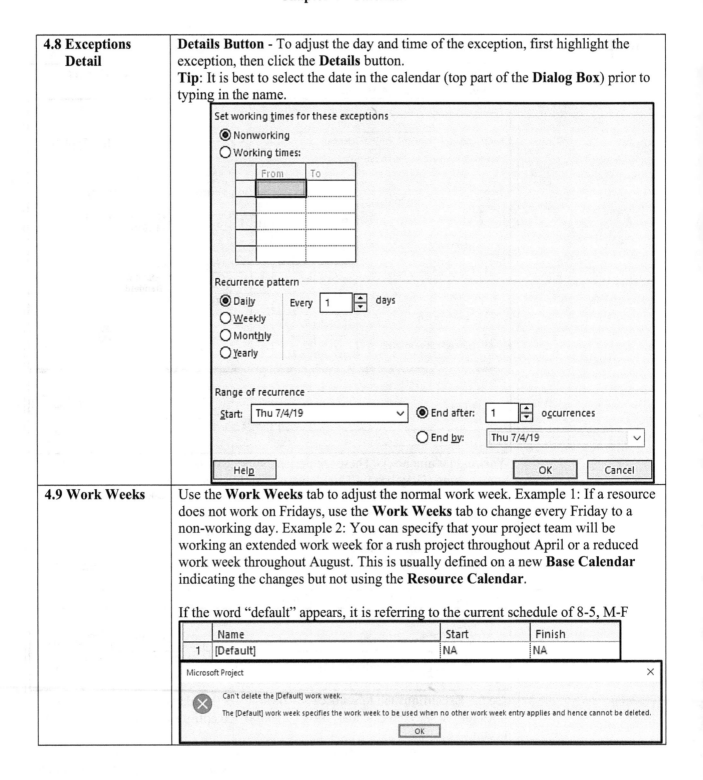
4.9 Work Weeks	Use the **Work Weeks** tab to adjust the normal work week. Example 1: If a resource does not work on Fridays, use the **Work Weeks** tab to change every Friday to a non-working day. Example 2: You can specify that your project team will be working an extended work week for a rush project throughout April or a reduced work week throughout August. This is usually defined on a new **Base Calendar** indicating the changes but not using the **Resource Calendar**. If the word "default" appears, it is referring to the current schedule of 8-5, M-F

4.10 Work Weeks Details	The Work Weeks Tab/Details Button will allow you to change work times for each day of the week such as Sunday, Monday, Tuesday, Wednesday, Thursday, Friday, and Saturday. 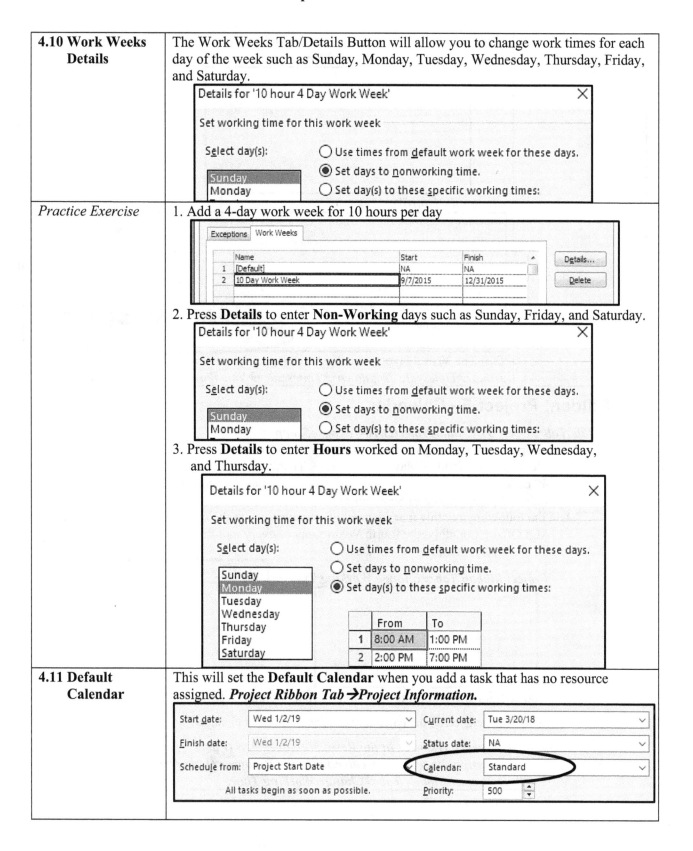
Practice Exercise	1. Add a 4-day work week for 10 hours per day 2. Press **Details** to enter **Non-Working** days such as Sunday, Friday, and Saturday. 3. Press **Details** to enter **Hours** worked on Monday, Tuesday, Wednesday, and Thursday.
4.11 Default Calendar	This will set the **Default Calendar** when you add a task that has no resource assigned. *Project Ribbon Tab→Project Information.*

4.12 Visible Calendar	This will allow you to see the calendar off days in gray in the Gantt Chart. *Right-Click on the timescale→Timescale.* 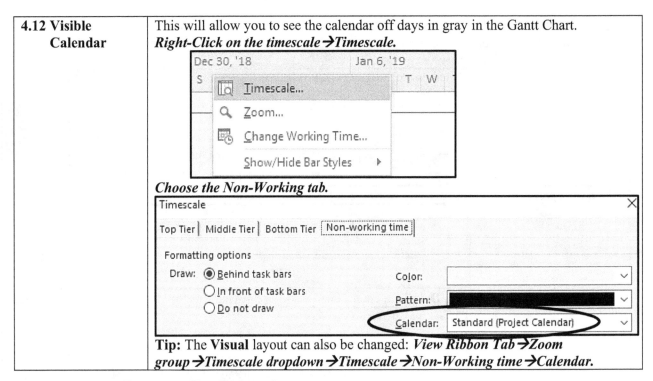 *Choose the Non-Working tab.*
	Tip: The **Visual** layout can also be changed: *View Ribbon Tab→Zoom group→Timescale dropdown→Timescale→Non-Working time→Calendar.*

Student Project F - Calendar

File Tab→Open→C:\Data\Project2016-1\House5.mpp
1. Add the appropriate holidays to the **Standard Calendar**:

Memorial Day (end of May)	Thanksgiving (end of November)
4th of July	Christmas (December 25)
Labor Day (beginning of September)	

Add the following monthly management offsite meetings to the calendar (Exception Tab):
Mgt Offsite (monthly, the fourth Wednesday of every month).
2. Create a secondary Contractor Calendar:

Project Ribbon Tab→Change Working Time→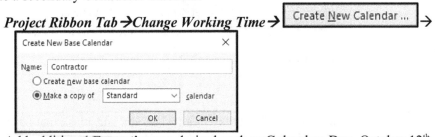

Add additional **Exceptions** as desired such as Columbus Day, October 12th.

When finished, close the calendar in order to save the changes.

3. *Optional: Create a resource in the Resource Sheet view (Laborer)*
Assign the secondary calendar to the Resource (Laborer)
Project Ribbon Tab→Change Working Time.

Change Working Time	
For calendar:	Laborer
Base calendar:	Contractor

Chapter 5 - Establishing Resources

In this chapter, we will establish or list resources needed and the standard rate of cost.

Concept	Explanation / *Command String in italic.*
5.1 Resource Sheet	This will define a list of available **Resources** in the **Resource Sheet**. *Task Ribbon Tab→Resource Sheet.*
5.2 Resource Name	This can be either a person's name, a general name defining the discipline, a material name, or an equipment name.
5.3 Resource Type	There are three types located in the **Type Column**: **Work** - A **Work Resource** can either be a person or equipment name such as John Johnson, Painter, or Crane. **Material** - This will define the **Material** or supplies used in the project. The **Material** is measured in units and each unit will have a label such as buckets, inches, Box of Tile, Square feet, etc. **Cost** - This is usually used for travel expenses. Since the name is usually "Travel Expense", no cost value needs to be entered in the **Resource Sheet**. However, when you assign the **Travel** name to a task, you can enter the **Travel Cost** amount at that time.
5.4 Material	This is a label used for **Material** units only. It is left blank when defining **Work** or **Cost Resources**. The label will contain units of measure such as buckets, lbs, inches, sq ft, etc.
5.5 Initials	This is generated from the name of the **Resource**. It is used for sorting and reference purposes only.
5.6 Group	The **Group** name will categorize common names. The **Group** name could be the subcontractor company grouping the employees, or it could be a general name providing names of organizations. This is primarily used to sort the **Resource List**.
5.7 Max	This represents the number of people related to the name of the **Resource**. Painters may state 500% which indicates 5 painters. One person can only be 100% or one person. If the person works part-time the value could be listed as 50%. **Tip:** This percentage value can also be listed as a number indicating the number of people in a group such as 5. To change this: *File Tab→Options→Schedule→*

5.8 Std. Rate	This is the wage or the amount to bill the project as hours are worked. It can be listed as 50/hr, 200/day, 50000/yr, etc. The system will use the value to calculate the hourly rate and bill accordingly.	Std. Rate ▼ $30.00/hr L00.00/day $40.00
5.9 Ovt. Rate	When hours exceed 40hrs per week (or the defined total hours), the **Overtime Rate** will begin charging to the project. If the employee is salaried and does not get paid **Overtime**, use the value of 0/hr.	Ovt. Rate ▼ $45.00/hr $0.00/hr
5.10 Cost/Use	This will charge the task the amount specified on a one-time only basis. It can be used for a setup fee needed to use the resource. An example is an employment agency fee, delivery charge for a crane, or any upfront cost to use the resource.	Cost/Use ▼ $0.00 $50.00 $0.00
5.11 Accrue Rate	This is the accounting method of adding costs to the project. **Start** - This means it will apply the cost of work performed at the start of the task. **Prorated** - This is the most common method which means it will apply cost as hours are used. **End** - This means the total cost will be applied at the end of the task or be billed when the job is complete.	Accrue At ▼ Prorated Prorated Start Prorated
5.12 Base Calendar	This is the **Base Calendar** used by the **Resource**. Each **Resource** can use a different **Base Calendar**. Usually, large groups will use a specialized **Base Calendar** defining holidays or work exceptions. The employees of a company may refer to one **Base Calendar** and contractors may refer to a different one.	Base Calendar ▼ Standard Standard
5.13 Code	This is an employee number, equipment ID, or identifier for the resource. It is only used for reference purposes and is not used in **Project** for any general purpose.	Code ▼ #12345
Practice Exercise	Enter the following resources: ***View Ribbon Tab→Resource Sheet***

Resource Name ▼	Type ▼	Material Label ▼	Initials ▼	Group ▼	Max. Units ▼	Std. Rate ▼	Ovt. Rate ▼	Cost/Use ▼	Accrue At ▼	Base Calendar ▼	Code ▼
Resource 1	Work		R	Contractor	100%	$30.00/hr	$45.00/hr	$0.00	Prorated	Standard	#12345
Equipment Rental	Work		E	Contractor	100%	L00.00/day	$0.00/hr	$50.00	Prorated	Standard	
Tile	Material	Box(50)	T	Supplies		$40.00		$0.00	Start		
Travel	Cost		T						Prorated		

5.14 Resource Calendar	When a **Work Resource** is created, a **Resource Calendar** is automatically created. After the **Resource** is created you can view the **Resource Calendar** at: ***Project Ribbon Tab→Change Working Time.*** **Note**: One common mistake made is that when the **Resource Calendar** is created in the **Change Working Time** screen, it has already been automatically created as the **Resource** is added.

5.15 Resource Information	This is a detailed view of the **Resource**. You can adjust the **Resource** availability and change in wages over the span of the project. This section will be covered in greater detail in the advanced class.
	
	Resource Information ✕
	General | Costs | Notes | Custom Fields |
	
	Resource name: Resource 1 Initials: R
	Email: Group: Contractor
	Logon Account... Code: #12345
	Booking type: Committed Type: Work
	   Material label:
	   ☐ Generic ☐ Budget
	Default Assignment Owner: ☐ Inactive
	Resource Availability
	
	Available From / Available To / Units
	1/1/2019 / 12/31/2019 / 100%
	Change Working Time ...

Practice Exercise	Set Resource1's availability: ***Resource Information → General Tab.*** Available From Available To Units 9/1/19 10/31/19 100% 11/1/19 12/31/19 0% (not available)
5.16 Resource Graph	The **Resource Graft** will show a column chart of employee usage and availability. The graph layout and fields displayed can be adjusted by: ***Format Ribbon Tab →*** ***Data Ribbon Group → Graph dropdown →*** Cost Cumulative Cost Cumulative Work Overallocation Peak Units Percent Allocation The Resources can be adjusted to different ones by pressing the right and left arrows under the **Resource Name**.
Practice Exercise	***View Ribbon Tab → Other Views → Resource Graph.***

Student Project G - Establishing Resources

File Tab→Open→C:\Data\Project2016-1\House5.mpp (Previously House6.mpp or House10).
Add the following resources to the **Resource Sheet:**

Task Ribbon Tab→ Gantt Dropdown→Resource Sheet.
Backhoe Operator (Type=Work, Group=Contractor, Max=200%, Std Rate=25, Ovt Rate=37)
Cable Specialist (Type=Work, Group=Contractor, Max=100%, Std Rate=18)
Backhoe (Type=Work, Group=Equipment, Std Rate=400/day)
Tile (Type=Material, Material=Square Feet, Group=Supplies, Std Rate=$4)
Concrete (Type=Material, Material=Yards, Group=Supplies, Std Rate=$80)

Optional
Superintendent (Type=Work, Group=Contractor, Max=100%, Std Rate=35, Ovt Rate=35)
Phone Technician (Type=Work, Group=Contractor, Max=100%, Std Rate=30)
Insulation (Type=Material, Material=Square Feet, Group=Supplies, Std Rate=$2)
Drywall (Type=Material, Material=Sheet, Group=Supplies, Std Rate=$8)
Change the contractor group to Calendar: Contractor

Chapter 6 - Assigning Resources

Once the resource has been added to the resource sheet, then assign the resource to a task.

Concept	Explanation / *Command String in italic.*
Practice Exercise 21	*Continue from the previous project (House10.mpp).*
6.1 Task Information	The **Task Information Dialog Box** can be used to **Assign Resources**. *Task Ribbon Tab→Information→Resource tab or Double click on the task to see the Task Information Dialog Box.* Task Information × General │ Predecessors │ Resources │ Advanced │ Notes │ Custom Fields │ Name: Task 1 Duration: 3 days ☐ Estimated Resources: Resource Name │ Assignment Owner │ Units │ Cost Resource1 │ │ 100% │ $720.00
6.2 Assign Resources	This is used to easily **Assign a Resource** to a task. You don't need to close the **Assign Resource Dialog Box**, just simply click on the next task. When **Assigning** two or more **Resources** to a task, be sure to select *all* **Resources** (using the Ctrl Key) prior to clicking the **Assign Button**. If you **Assign** them one at a time, it may adjust the **Duration**. *Resource Ribbon Tab→Assign Resources.* Assign Resources Task: Task 1 Resource list options Resources from 5-123456.mpp Resource Name │ R/D │ Units │ Cost ✓ Resource1 │ │ 100% │ $720.00 Equipment Rental Tile Travel Assign │ Remove │ Replace... │ Graph
6.3 Resource Names Column	**Resources** can be assigned in the **Resource Name Column**. To see the **Resource Name Column**, expand the table area by moving the slider bar to the right. Resource Names ▼ │ T │ F Resource1 ∨ ☐ Equipment Rental ☑ Resource1 ☐ Tile ☐ Travel Predecessor ▼ │ Resource Names │ Jun 7, '15 W │ S Surveyor[200%] │ Surveyor[2 Expand Slider ...ting Specialist

Practice Exercise Assign Resources	1. Create a blank Project: *File Tab→New→Blank Project.*
	2. Add several tasks: *View Ribbon Tab→Gantt Chart→*
	    Task Name: Enter Task1, Task2, Task3, etc.
	3. Add several resources to the **Resource Sheet**:
	    View Ribbon Tab→Resource Sheet→Enter In Resource, 1, Resource2, etc.
	4. Use the 3 methods above to add resources to the tasks.

6.4 Task Type	This is a calculation method used to change the characteristics of **Work** (hours), **Duration**, and **Units** (number of people assigned). If **Fixed Duration** is checked, that will mean as people are added to the task, the duration will not change. When **Fixed Units** (default) is used, it will change the **Duration** of a task as more people are added. *Task Information→Advanced Tab→Task Type→* **Fixed Duration** - Units and Work may change, but **Duration** will remain fixed. **Fixed Units** - Duration and Work may change, but **Units** will remain fixed. **Fixed Work** - Units and Duration may change, but **Work** will remain fixed. Task type: Fixed Units ∨ ☐ Effort driven

Student Project H - Assigning Resources
File Tab→Open →C:\Data\Project2016-1\House7.mpp.
Add the following assignments using each of the techniques listed above.

Task Name	Duration	Gantt / Resource Assignment
Conduct Site Survey	1 day	Surveyor[200%]
Develop Blueprints	2 wks	Architect
Draft Proposal	5 days	Contracting Specialist
Request Bids	1 wk	Contracting Specialist
Request Permits	1 day	Contracting Specialist
Obtain Permits	1 wk	Contracting Specialist
Obtain Bids	1 wk	Contracting Specialist[50%],Superintendent[50%]
Select Subcontractors	1 wk	Superintendent
Complete Planning Phase	0 days	7/29
▲ Build Structure	38.56 days	
▲ Build Foundation	5.56 days	
Dig Foundation	3 days	Backhoe Operator[200%],Backhoe[200%]
Smooth Foundation	2.5 days	Backhoe Operator[200%],Backhoe[200%]
Pour Foundation	1 day	Laborer,Concrete[40 yards]
▲ Construct Frame	9 days	
Frame House	6 days	Carpenter[300%]
Frame Garage	3 days	Carpenter[200%]
Install Roof	1 wk	Roofer[200%],Roofing Materials[1]
Install Doors	3 days	Laborer[200%],Doors[10 units]
Install Windows	3.5 days	Laborer[200%],Windows[24 units]
Install Siding	1 wk	Laborer[200%],Siding Materials[1]
Build Deck	3 days	Carpenter[200%]
▲ Build Infrastructure	39 days	
Initial Plumbing	7 days	Plumber[200%]
Initial Electricity	2 wks	Electrician[300%]
Security System	1 day	
Install Cable	1 day	Cable Specialist
Run Phone Lines	1 day	Phone Technician
Insulation	4 days	Laborer[300%],Insulation[3,000 square feet]
Drywall	4 days	Laborer[200%],Drywall[170 sheets]
Painting	3 days	Painter[400%],Paint[20 gallons]
Flooring	1 wk	Laborer[200%],Tile[350 square feet]
Final Plumbing	3 days	Plumber,Plumbing Supplies[1]
Final Electric	3 days	Electrician[200%],Light Fixtures[1]

Chapter 7 - Leveling Resources

Here, we will cover the most common techniques and identify and fix **Over-Allocated Resources**. When **Resources** are double booked, or two tasks occur at the same time using the same **Resource**, the **Resource Over-Allocation** will need to be corrected. This can be done automatically by using the **Leveling Tool**.

Concept	Explanation / *Command String in italic.*
Practice Exercise 22	*File tab →Open → C:\Data\Project2016-1\House8.mpp.*
7.1 Resource Usage	The **Resource Usage** screen is used to identify **Over-Allocated** resources. *Task Ribbon Tab→Gantt Chart drop-down→Resource Usage.* **Tip**: the Gantt Chart will look similar to the following:
7.2 Leveling Techniques	The following are techniques that can be used to **Level** or fix an **Over-Allocated Resource**. **Resource Leveling** - This is an automatic tool used to fix **Resource** problems. *Resource →Level Resource/Leveling Options.* **Change Relationship** - This technique is a manual method used to change the relationship of tasks such as changing a **Start-To-Start** relationship to a **Finish-To-Start** relationship. **Change Lead/Lag** - This is used to remove a **Lead** or **Lag** that caused a resource to be **Over-Allocated**. A more common example is a **Lead** that overlaps two tasks. **Add Additional Resources** - This is used to add **Additional Resources** to the **Resource Sheet** if the **Resource Usage** indicates that you do not have enough assigned **Resources**. **Reassign The Resource** - This is used to eliminate **Over-Allocation** issues by assigning an **Under-Allocated Resource** to an **Over-Allocated Resource**.

7.3 Three Windows	In order to resolve resource problems, you may need to view multiple windows. This will create a new **Window** for the **Resource Sheet, Gantt Chart**, and **Resource Usage Views**. You will then switch to a different window to view any encountered and solve issues.
	1. **Gantt Chart View**
	   It is assumed that **Project** is opened and displaying the **Gantt Chart View**.
	2. **Resource Sheet View:**
	
	   View Ribbon Tab➔ New Window➔View: Resource Sheet.
	
	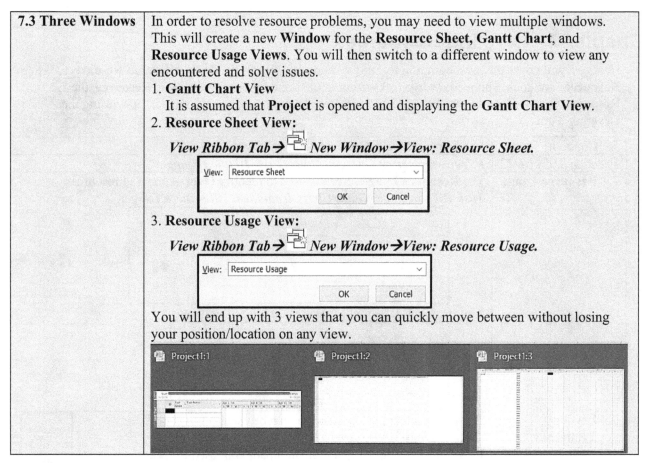
	
	3. **Resource Usage View:**
	
	   View Ribbon Tab➔ New Window➔View: Resource Usage.
	
	You will end up with 3 views that you can quickly move between without losing your position/location on any view.

Student Project I - Leveling

Fix the following **Over-Allocated Resource** problems:

File Tab➔Open➔C:\Data\Project2016-1\House8.mpp

Hint: Use *View Ribbon Tab➔Windows Group➔New Window* to add the above windows to House8.mpp. Add windows **Resource Sheet**, **Resource Usage**, and the **Gantt Chart**.

Student Project I1 - Leveling Technique

1. Identify **Resource Over-Allocation**: *View Ribbon Tab➔Resource Usage View➔*
   Select Labor/Install Windows task➔
   Task Ribbon Tab➔Scroll to the task.

ⓘ	Resource Name	Work	Details	M	T	W	T
👤	⊿ Laborer	488 hrs	Work	32h	24h	16h	16h
	Pour Foundation	8 hrs	Work				
	Install Doors	48 hrs	Work	16h	8h		
	Install Windows	64 hrs	Work	16h	16h	16h	8h

2. Level the Resource: *Resource Ribbon Tab →Level group →Level Resources →*
   Select Laborer →Level Now button.

3. **Resource Usage** will look similar to the following:

	Resource Name ▾	Work ▾	Details	M	T	W	T
ⓘ	◢ Laborer	488 hrs	Work	16h	16h	16h	16h
	Pour Foundation	8 hrs	Work				
	Install Doors	48 hrs	Work	16h	8h		
	Install Windows	64 hrs	Work	0h	8h	16h	16h

Student Project I2 - Add More Resources Technique
1. To identify the over-allocation: *View Ribbon Tab →Resource Usage View →*
   Select Painter/Painting task →Task Ribbon Tab → Scroll to task →
   (note that 32 h requires 4 Painters).

	◢ Painter	96 hrs	Work	16h	32h	32h	16h
	Painting	96 hrs	Work	16h	32h	32h	16h

2. To Solve the over-allocation: *View Ribbon Tab →Resource Sheet →*
   Review the Max Column to determine the hours needed.

	Painter	Work		P	Union	300%

3. Resource Sheet view: *Painter →Change to 400%.*
   The result should look similar to the following:

	Painter	Work		P	Union	400%

Student Project I3 - Change Relationship Technique
1. To identify the over-allocation: ***Resource Usage View*** →
   Select Contracting Specialist/Obtain Bids task→Task Ribbon Tab→Scroll to the task.

	⊿ Contracting Specialist	120 hrs	Work	8h	8h	8h	12h	12h
	Draft Proposal	24 hrs	Work					
	Request Bids	40 hrs	Work	8h				
	Request Permits	8 hrs	Work		8h			
	Obtain Permits	40 hrs	Work			8h	8h	8h
	Obtain Bids	8 hrs	Work			0h	4h	4h

2. To fix the over-allocation: ***Gantt chart view→Select Obtain Bids*** →
   Scroll to task→ Select the link between Obtain Permits/Obtain Bids

	Obtain Permits	1 wk	▭ Contracting Specialist
	Obtain Bids	2 days	▭ Contracting Specialist[50%],Sup

3. Change the relationship: ***Change the Task Dependency screen to Finish-To-Start(FS)***
   Change the Lag to 0d

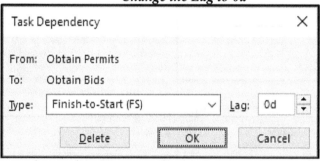

4. Observe the results: ***Resource Usage view to review results***

	Obtain Permits	1 wk	▭ Contracting Specialist
	Obtain Bids	2 days	▭ Contracting Specialist[50%],

5. Observe the Resource Usage View: ***View Ribbon Tab→ Resource Usage View→***
   Select Contracting Specialist/Obtain Bids task→Task Ribbon Tab→Scroll to task

	⊿ Contracting Specialist	120 hrs	Work	8h	8h	4h	4h	
	Draft Proposal	24 hrs	Work					
	Request Bids	40 hrs	Work					
	Request Permits	8 hrs	Work					
	Obtain Permits	40 hrs	Work	8h	8h			
	Obtain Bids	8 hrs	Work		0h	4h	4h	

Student Project I4 - Lead/Lag Technique
1. To identify the over-allocation: ***Resource Usage View→Select Carpenter/Frame***
   Garage task→Task Ribbon Tab→Scroll to task→

	⊿ Carpenter	240 hrs	Work	32h	40h	28h	8h	
	Frame House	144 hrs	Work	24h	24h	12h		
	Frame Garage	48 hrs	Work	8h	16h	16h	8h	

2. To resolve the over-allocation: *View Ribbon Tab→Gantt Chart view→*
Select Frame House→Scroll to task→the Select relationship between Frame House and
Frame Garage.

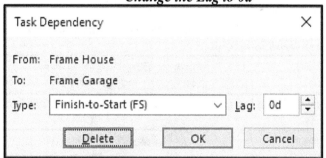

3. Change the relationship: *Change the Task Dependency screen to Finish-To-Start(FS)*
Change the Lag to 0d

Task Dependency	✕
From: Frame House	
To: Frame Garage	
Type: Finish-to-Start (FS) ▾	Lag: 0d ▴▾
Delete	OK	Cancel

4. Observe the results: *Resource Usage view to review results*

⊿ Construct Frame	9 days					
Frame House	6 days				Carpenter[300%]
Frame Garage	3 days				Carpenter[200%]

5. Observe the Resource Usage View: *View Ribbon Tab→ Resource Usage View→*
Select Carpenter/Frame Garage task →Task Ribbon Tab→Scroll to the task.

⊿ Carpenter	240 hrs	Work	24h	24h	20h	16h	16h
Frame House	144 hrs	Work	24h	24h	12h		
Frame Garage	48 hrs	Work			8h	16h	16h

Student Project I5 - Lead/Lag

1. To identify the over-allocation: *Resource Usage View→Select Backhoe Operator/Smooth*
Foundation task→ Task Ribbon Tab→Scroll to task→

2. To resolve the over-allocation: *View Ribbon Tab→ Gantt Chart view→Select Smooth*
Foundation → Scroll to task→Select the relationship between the Backhoe Operator
and Smooth Foundation

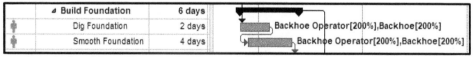

3. Change the relationship: *Change the Lag to 0d.*

Task Dependency	✕
From: Dig Foundation	
To: Smooth Foundation	
Type: Finish-to-Start (FS) ▾	Lag: 0d ▴▾
Delete	OK	Cancel

4: Observe the results: ***Resource Usage view to review results.***

◢ Build Foundation	7 days	
Dig Foundation	2 days	Backhoe Operator[200%],Backhoe[200%]
Smooth Foundation	4 days	Backhoe Operator[200%],Backhoe[200%]

5. Observe the Resource Usage View: ***View Ribbon Tab→ Resource Usage View→ Select Backhoe Operator/Smooth Foundation task →Task Ribbon Tab→Scroll to task.***

◢ Backhoe Operator	96 hrs	Work	8h	16h		16h	16h	16h	16h	8h
Dig Foundation	32 hrs	Work	8h	16h		8h				
Smooth Foundation	64 hrs	Work				8h	16h	16h	16h	8h

Student Project I6 - Split Task

1. Identify the task to split: ***Gantt Chart View→Select Landscaping Task→ Task Ribbon Tab→Scroll to task→***

Landscaping	1 wk	Landscaper	
Cement Work	2 days	Laborer[300%],Concrete[15 yards]	

2. ***Task Ribbon Tab→Split Task→Click just above the "Cement Work" task on the Landscaping task.***

Landscaping	1 wk	Landscaper	
Cement Work	2 days	Laborer[300%],Concrete[15 yards]	

3. The result will look similar to the following:

Tip: You might need to attempt this several times by pressing **Undo** and trying again.

Landscaping	1 wk	Landscaper	
Cement Work	2 days	Laborer[300%],Concrete[15 yards]	

If the result is not wide enough, you can choose the **Split Task** and stretch **the Split** similar to the following:

Landscaping	1 wk	Landscaper	
Cement Work	2 days	Laborer[300%],Concrete[15 yards]	

Tip: You may receive this help message guiding you through the process:

Split Task:	
Scheduled Start:	Mon 11/18/19
Click to insert a split on the task.	

Chapter 8 - Cost

The **Cost** of a task or overall project is calculated and displayed. This is useful to determine if the allocated funds are sufficient to complete a project. Also, it is useful to determine if the project is on track.

Concept	Explanation / *Command String in italic.*
Practice Exercise 23	*Continue from Previous Project (House8.mpp).*
8.1 Statistics	This shows the overall cost of the project. ***Project Ribbon Tab→Project Information→Statistics.***

Project Statistics for 'HOUSE9.mpp'   ×

	Start	Finish
Current	Wed 6/5/19	Fri 11/22/19
Baseline	NA	NA
Actual	NA	NA
Variance	0d	0d

	Duration	Work	Cost
Current	123d	1,905.25h	$51,728.00
Baseline	0d	0h	$0.00
Actual	0d	0h	$0.00
Remaining	123d	1,905.25h	$51,728.00

Concept	Explanation
8.2 Cost Table	The **Cost Table** displays the **Cost** of each task. In **Gantt Chart View**: *View Ribbon Tab→Table drop-down→Cost.*

Task Name	Fixed Cost	Fixed Cost Accrual	Total Cost	Baseline	Variance	Actual	Remaining
Conduct Site Survey	$0.00	Prorated	$1,440.00	$0.00	$1,440.00	$0.00	$1,440.00
Develop Blueprints	$0.00	Prorated	$4,680.00	$0.00	$4,680.00	$0.00	$4,680.00
Draft Proposal	$0.00	Prorated	$648.00	$0.00	$648.00	$0.00	$648.00
Request Bids	$0.00	Prorated	$1,080.00	$0.00	$1,080.00	$0.00	$1,080.00
Request Permits	$0.00	Prorated	$216.00	$0.00	$216.00	$0.00	$216.00
Obtain Permits	$0.00	Prorated	$1,080.00	$0.00	$1,080.00	$0.00	$1,080.00
Obtain Bids	$0.00	Prorated	$216.00	$0.00	$216.00	$0.00	$216.00

Concept	Explanation
8.3 Resource Rate	The **Resource Sheet** view shows the Standard Rate, Overtime Rate, and Cost Per Use. This value times the task hours will calculate the total task cost.

Std. Rate ▼	Ovt. Rate ▼	Cost/Use ▼
$20.00/hr	$30.00/hr	$0.00
$18.00/hr	$27.00/hr	$0.00
$30.00/hr	$45.00/hr	$0.00

Concept	Explanation
8.4 Summary	The **Summary** sheet will display the **Cost Column**. In **Gantt Chart View**: *View Ribbon Tab→Table drop-down→Summary.*

Task Name	Duration	Start	Finish	% Comp.	Cost	Work
Conduct Site Survey	1 day	Fri 6/5/15	Fri 6/5/15	0%	$580.00	16 hrs
Develop Blueprints	2 wks	Mon 6/8/15	Fri 6/19/15	0%	$4,780.00	72 hrs
Draft Proposal	5 days	Mon 6/22/15	Fri 6/26/15	0%	$1,080.00	40 hrs
Request Bids	1 wk	Mon 6/29/15	Fri 7/3/15	0%	$1,080.00	40 hrs

Tip: If you are in the **Resource Sheet View**, you will receive a similar layout.

	In **Resource Sheet View**: *View Ribbon Tab →Table drop-down →Summary.*

Resource Name	Group	Max.	Peak	Std. Rate	Ovt. Rate	Cost	Work
Laborer	Union	300%	300%	$20.00/hr	$30.00/hr	$9,760.00	488 hrs
Painter	Union	400%	400%	$18.00/hr	$27.00/hr	$1,728.00	96 hrs
Electrician	Union	300%	300%	$30.00/hr	$45.00/hr	$8,640.00	288 hrs
Plumber	Union	200%	200%	$50.00/hr	$75.00/hr	$6,800.00	136 hrs
Surveyor	Contractor	200%	200%	$30.00/hr	$45.00/hr	$1,440.00	48 hrs
Contracting Specialist	Contractor	100%	100%	$27.00/hr	$40.50/hr	$3,240.00	120 hrs
Architect	Contractor	100%	100%	$65.00/hr	$0.00/hr	$4,680.00	72 hrs

8.5 Project Summary

This will add a **Project Summary** task on the top of the table names and will summarize the entire list. The Cost Column will display the total **Project Cost**. *Format Ribbon Tab → ☑ Project Summary →Right-Click on Start → Insert Column →Cost.*

Task Name	Duration	Start	Finish	% Comp.	Cost	Work
◢ C:\Proj2k\M2\NewM2	123 days	Wed 6/5/19	Fri 11/22/19	0%	$51,728.00	1,905.25 hrs
Conduct Site Survey	3 days	Wed 6/5/19	Fri 6/7/19	0%	$1,440.00	48 hrs
Develop Blueprints	2 wks	Mon 6/10/19	Fri 6/21/19	0%	$4,680.00	72 hrs
Draft Proposal	3 days	Mon 6/24/19	Wed 6/26/19	0%	$648.00	24 hrs
Request Bids	1 wk	Thu 6/27/19	Wed 7/3/19	0%	$1,080.00	40 hrs
Request Permits	1 day	Thu 7/4/19	Thu 7/4/19	0%	$216.00	8 hrs
Obtain Permits	1 wk	Fri 7/5/19	Thu 7/11/19	0%	$1,080.00	40 hrs
Obtain Bids	2 days	Fri 7/12/19	Tue 7/16/19	0%	$216.00	17.25 hrs
Select Subcontractors	1 wk	Tue 7/16/19	Mon 7/22/19	0%	$0.00	40 hrs
Complete Planning Phas	0 days	Mon 7/22/19	Mon 7/22/19	0%	$0.00	0 hrs
◢ Build Structure	41 days	Mon 7/22/19	Tue 9/17/19	0%	$10,600.00	712 hrs
◢ Build Foundation	8 days	Mon 7/22/19	Thu 8/1/19	0%	$160.00	200 hrs

8.6 Accrual Methods

The **Costs** will be adjusted based on the **Accrual Method** chosen in the **Resource Sheet**.
Accrual Beginning – This will calculate the entire **Task Cost** at beginning
Accrual End – This will calculate the entire **Task Cost** at the end of the task.
Accrual Prorated – This uses successive points to calculate the **Cost** of the **Task**.

8.7 Resource Rate Table	The **Cost** of a task can be affected by the cost changes in the **Resource Information Dialog Box**. *Resource Sheet→Resource Information→Cost Tab.* The following shows a standard rate change of 6/3/2019. Any task that falls after this date will be billed at the new rate.

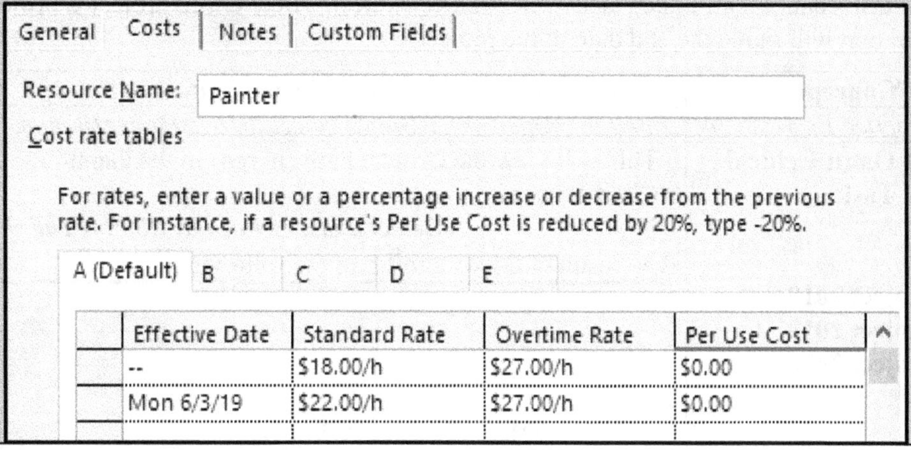

General | Costs | Notes | Custom Fields

Resource Name: Painter

Cost rate tables

For rates, enter a value or a percentage increase or decrease from the previous rate. For instance, if a resource's Per Use Cost is reduced by 20%, type -20%.

A (Default) | B | C | D | E

	Effective Date	Standard Rate	Overtime Rate	Per Use Cost	^
	--	$18.00/h	$27.00/h	$0.00	
	Mon 6/3/19	$22.00/h	$27.00/h	$0.00	

Student Project J - Cost

Continue from the previous Project (House9.mpp).
Analyze the cost by reviewing the following:
Project Ribbon Tab→Project Information→Statistics.
View Ribbon Tab→Table dropdown→Cost.

Determine the three highest-cost tasks.
Add $200 to the **Survey** task in the **Fixed Cost Column**.

Chapter 9 - Critical Path

A **Critical Path** is a series of tasks usually assigned a **Finish-To-Finish** relationship. As a result, when one task changes, all linked tasks will change, as well. If the entire project is critical, then a change in the Duration will move the end date of the project.

Concept	Explanation / *Command String in italic.*
Practice Exercise 24	*File tab →Open → C:\Data\Project2016-1\House10.mpp.*
9.1 Gantt Critical Task **Project 2010** **Project 2013** **Project 2016**	This will view the Critical Path (in red) in the Gantt Chart View. ☑ Critical Tasks ☑ Slack ***Select a task →Format Ribbon Tab →*** The result will look similar to the following: **Task Name / Duration** Conduct Site Survey — 3 days Develop Blueprints — 2 wks Draft Proposal — 3 days Request Bids — 1 wk Request Permits — 1 day Obtain Permits — 1 wk Obtain Bids — 2 days Select Subcontractor — 1 wk
9.2 Detailed Gantt	The **Detailed Gantt** view will show the **Critical Path** in red, similar to the **Critical Tasks** check box. *Task Ribbon Tab →Gantt Chart drop-down →More Views →Detailed Gantt view.* **Task Name / Duration** Conduct Site Survey — 3 days Develop Blueprints — 2 wks Draft Proposal — 3 days Request Bids — 1 wk Request Permits — 1 day Obtain Permits — 1 wk Obtain Bids — 2 days Select Subcontractor — 1 wk
9.3 Schedule	The **Schedule** will show the numeric result of the **Critical Path**. The **Start/Finish** dates are the currently scheduled dates, and the **Late Start/Late Finish** dates are the latest a task can be scheduled without affecting other tasks. **Free Slack** is the difference between the **Start** and **Late Finish** dates. The **Total Slack** is how far all tasks can change until the end date of the project is changed. *View Ribbon Tab →Table drop-down →Schedule.*

Task Name	Start	Finish	Late Start	Late Finish	Free Slack	Total Slack
Conduct Site Survey	Wed 6/5/19	Fri 6/7/19	Wed 6/5/19	Fri 6/7/19	0 days	0 days
Develop Blueprints	Mon 6/10/19	Fri 6/21/19	Mon 6/10/19	Fri 6/21/19	0 wks	0 wks
Draft Proposal	Mon 6/24/19	Wed 6/26/19	Mon 6/24/19	Wed 6/26/19	0 days	0 days
Request Bids	Thu 6/27/19	Wed 7/3/19	Thu 6/27/19	Wed 7/3/19	0 wks	0 wks
Request Permits	Thu 7/4/19	Thu 7/4/19	Thu 7/4/19	Thu 7/4/19	0 days	0 days
Obtain Permits	Fri 7/5/19	Thu 7/11/19	Fri 7/5/19	Thu 7/11/19	0 wks	0 wks
Obtain Bids	Fri 7/12/19	Tue 7/16/19	Mon 7/15/19	Tue 7/16/19	0 days	0 days
Select Subcontractors	Tue 7/16/19	Mon 7/22/19	Tue 7/16/19	Mon 7/22/19	0 wks	0 wks

9.4 Slack	**Slack** is the amount a task can slip until the linked successor task begins to change. To build in **Slack**, use a constraint to push the successor task to the future. The following shows one day of slack:
Practice Exercise 25 Add Slack	To add **Slack** to a task, open the **Task Information** screen and add a projected date to the **Constraint** of **Start-No-Earlier-Than**. 1. Create the following and change the tasks to be **Auto-Schedule:**

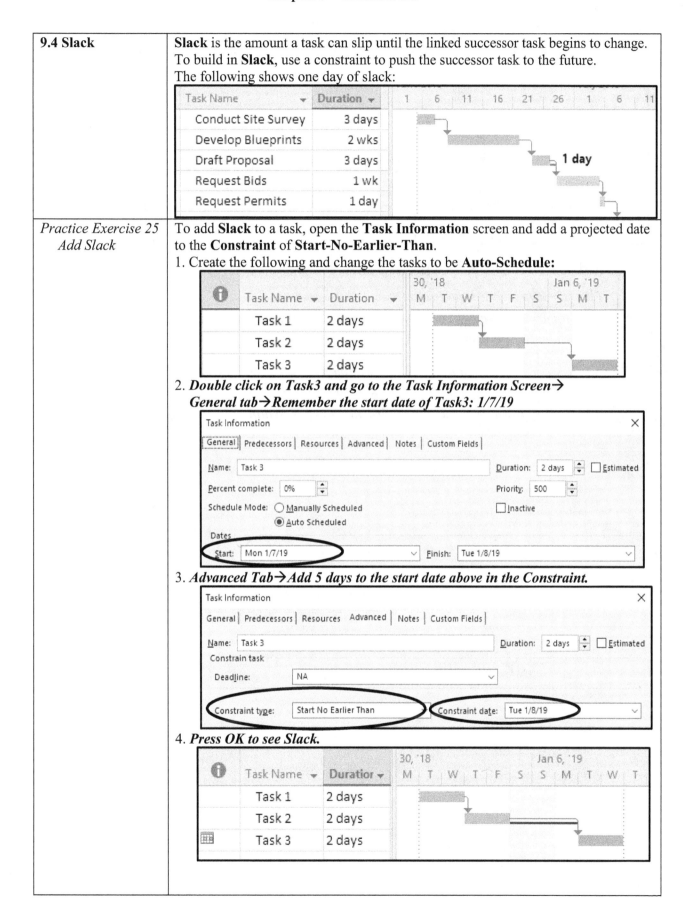

2. *Double click on Task3 and go to the Task Information Screen→ General tab→Remember the start date of Task3: 1/7/19*

3. *Advanced Tab→Add 5 days to the start date above in the Constraint.*

4. *Press OK to see Slack.*

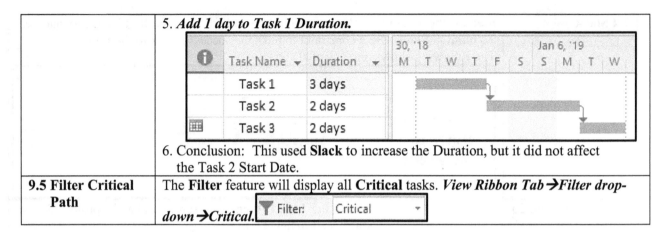

	5. *Add 1 day to Task 1 Duration.*
	6. Conclusion: This used **Slack** to increase the Duration, but it did not affect the Task 2 Start Date.
9.5 Filter Critical Path	The **Filter** feature will display all **Critical** tasks. *View Ribbon Tab→Filter drop-down→Critical.* ▼ Filter: Critical ▼

Student Project K - Critical Path

File Tab→Open→C:\Data\Project2016-1\House10.mpp

Task Ribbon Tab→Gantt Chart dropdown→More Views→Detailed Gantt.
Review the critical path in red.

Add Slack to the "Install Roof" task by adding five days to the "Install Doors" task. Increase the Install Roof duration to eight days.

Add Slack of five days to the drywall task to ensure everything will be complete prior to installing the drywall.

Chapter 10 - Baseline/Intern Plan

A **Baseline** will take a picture of the project and record the duration, start, and finish. You can use this information at a later time to compare the progress of the project.

Concept	Explanation / *Command String in italic.*
Practice Exercise 26	*Continue from the previous project (House10.mpp).*
10.1 Set Baseline	This will set the **Baseline**. 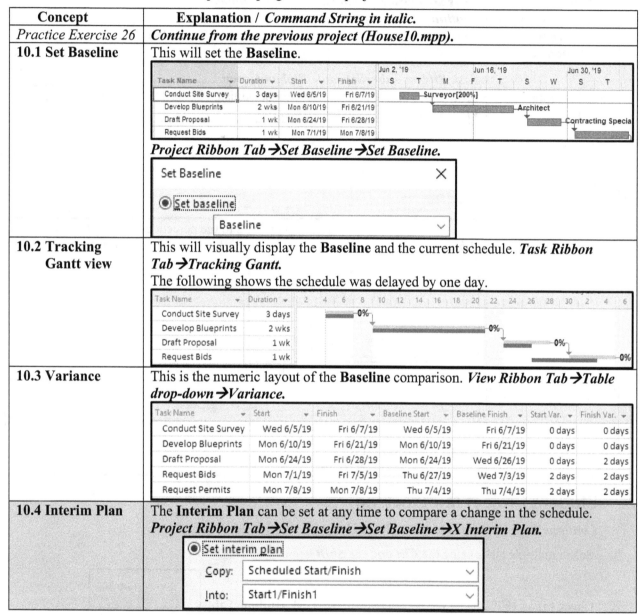
10.2 Tracking Gantt view	This will visually display the **Baseline** and the current schedule. *Task Ribbon Tab→Tracking Gantt.* The following shows the schedule was delayed by one day.
10.3 Variance	This is the numeric layout of the **Baseline** comparison. *View Ribbon Tab→Table drop-down→Variance.*
10.4 Interim Plan	The **Interim Plan** can be set at any time to compare a change in the schedule. *Project Ribbon Tab→Set Baseline→Set Baseline→X Interim Plan.*

Student Project L - Baseline

Continue from the previous project (House10.mpp).
Project Ribbon Tab→Set Baseline→Set Baseline.
Task Ribbon Tab→Tracking Gantt.
View Ribbon Tab→Table dropdown→Variance.

Chapter 11 - Tracking

In this chapter, we will check tasks to be partially or 100% complete.

Concept	Explanation / *Command String in italic.*
Practice Exercise 28	***Continue from the previous project (House10.mpp)***
11.1 Percent Complete	The completion of a task can be adjusted in the **Task Ribbon Tab**: *Task Ribbon Tab→Schedule Ribbon Group.*
11.2 Tracking Table	Setting the completion of a task can be adjusted in the **Tracking Table**. *View Ribbon Tab→Tables→Tracking.*

	Task Name	Act. Start	Act. Finish	% Comp.	Phys. % Comp.	Act. Dur.	Rem. Dur.	Act. Cost	Act. Work
1	Conduct Site Survey	Wed 6/5/19	Fri 6/7/19	100%	0%	3 days	0 days	$1,440.00	48 hrs
2	Develop Blueprints	Mon 6/10/19	Fri 6/21/19	100%	0%	2 wks	0 wks	$4,680.00	72 hrs
3	Draft Proposal	Mon 6/24/19	Fri 6/28/19	100%	0%	1 wk	0 wks	$1,080.00	40 hrs
4	Request Bids	Mon 7/1/19	NA	50%	0%	0.5 wks	0.5 wks	$540.00	20 hrs
5	Request Permits	NA	NA	0%	0%	0 days	1 day	$0.00	0 hrs

11.3 Gantt Percentage

This will change the status next to the bars to the percent complete: *Format Ribbon Tab→Format drop-down button→Bar Styles→Text Tab (located on the bottom).*

Text	Bars
Left	
Right	% Complete

The result will look similar to the following:

	ⓘ	Task Name	Duration	
1	✓	Conduct Site Survey	3 days	100%
2	✓	Develop Blueprints	2 wks	100%
3	✓	Draft Proposal	1 wk	100%
4		Request Bids	1 wk	50%
5		Request Permits	1 day	0%

Student Project M - Tracking

Continue from a previous project (House10.mpp).

Select multiple tasks using the ***Ctrl and the Shift keys.***

Check off as **100%** using the percentages in the **Task Ribbon Tab**

Check off a task at **50%** to see the result in the **Gantt Chart View.**

Chapter 12 - Reporting

Reports are used to extract information from the **Project**. There are **Visual Reports** which are extracted and displayed in **Excel**. Regular reports to show status/progress, and a **Print** of the project screen. Reports are very different in **Project 2013** compared to **Project 2010**.

Chapter Contents

Section 1 - Regular Project Reports

Concept	Explanation / *Command String in italic.*
Practice Exercise 29	Continue from the previous project (**House10.mpp**).
12.1 Reports 2016 **Project 2016**	
12.2 Reports 2013 **Project 2013**	One of the major changes to **Project 2013** is that the new **Reports Ribbon Tab** and **Reporting** option have been enhanced.
12.3 Reports 2010 **Project 2010**	Located in *Project→Reports Ribbon Group*:
12.4 Custom Reports	This is used to customize existing **Reports**. **Project 2010**: *Project Ribbon Tab→Reports→(Select Report)→Edit* existing report and *Project Ribbon Tab→Reports→Custom Report* **Project 2013/2016**: *Reports Ribbon Tab→Reports→(Select Report)→Edit* existing report and *Reports Ribbon Tab→Reports→Custom Report*

Section 2 - Visual Reports

Concept	Explanation / *Command String in italic.*
12.5 Visual Reports **Project 2016**	*Reports Ribbon Tab→View Reports Group →Visual Reports* 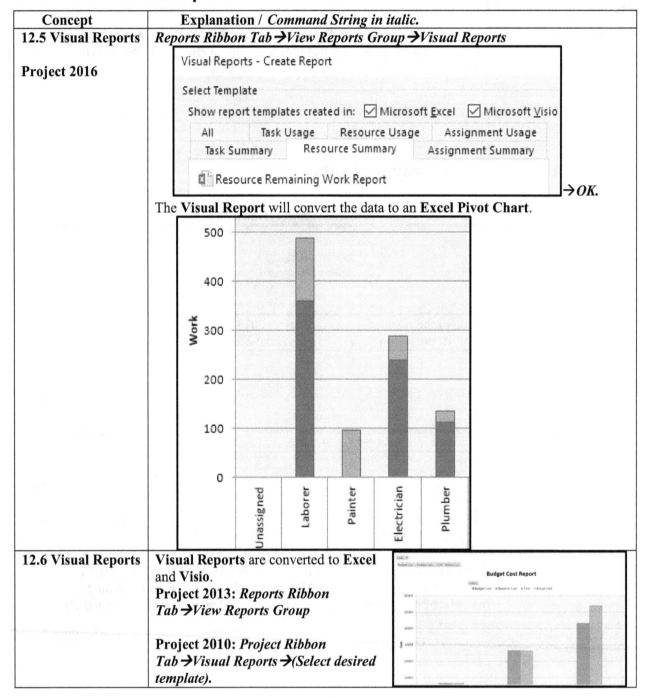 →*OK.* The **Visual Report** will convert the data to an **Excel Pivot Chart**.
12.6 Visual Reports	**Visual Reports** are converted to **Excel** and **Visio**. **Project 2013:** *Reports Ribbon Tab→View Reports Group* **Project 2010:** *Project Ribbon Tab→Visual Reports→(Select desired template).*

Section 3 - Project Printing

Concept	Explanation / *Command String in italic.*
12.7 Printing	This will **Print** out what is displayed on the screen. *File Tab→Print→Page Setup→ Headers/Footers/Legend* (Remove the legend). Header/Footer/Legend (Insert Logo) *File Tab→Print→X Print left column of pages only.*
12.8 Copy Picture	This will make a **Copy** of the current screen for status report purposes. *Task Ribbon Tab→Copy drop-down→Copy Picture.*
12.9 PDF Printing	Project 2013: Print to PDF. *File tab→Save As Adobe PDF.* Project 2010: Print to PDF. *File tab→Save As Adobe PDF.*

Student Project N - Reporting

There are several ways to **Print** a **Project to PDF**. This may change in the different versions of **Project** or depend on if additional **PDF** add-ins were applied to your installation of **Project**. Test out which method is supported on your computer.

Run several **Visual Reports:** *Project Ribbon Tab→Visual Reports.*
    Run several reports: *Project Ribbon Tab→Visual Reports.*
    Do a **Print Preview** of the Gantt Chart: *File Tab→Print.*
    Test out the **Copy Picture** feature: *Task Ribbon Tab→Copy drop-down→Copy Picture.*

Final Project - Newsletter Case Study

You have just agreed to take on the job of publishing a company newsletter that will be distributed to the 3000 employees in your organization. You have two assistants, Mary and Fred, who work for you. They each earn $12.00 per hour. Your salary is $50,000 per year. You have other commitments in your job but you will be able to spend from 8:00 a.m. till noon each day on the newsletter project. Both Mary and Fred can spend full time.

The newsletter will contain:
- 3 full-length articles
- A president's message
- 4 mini articles
- A flyer describing the Christmas party
- A party RSVP form that can be emailed or mailed
- 3 advertisement spaces that will sell for $100 each
- Postage and Printing will cost $3,000

Later today you have to make a presentation to your management and convince them that it is feasible to try and get the December issue out by the Thursday after Thanksgiving. Management is willing to start publishing the newsletter in January, but you feel that the holiday issue would be a good kickoff for your new position as editor. Management also wants to know what the real cost of publishing this newsletter will be.

Assumptions and Constraints
- Today is the first Monday in November.
- Thanksgiving and the day after are holidays for everyone.
- The printer is closed for the entire Thanksgiving weekend
  - (Thursday through Sunday).
- You are willing to work the day after Thanksgiving if necessary.
- Mary is taking the whole week of Thanksgiving
  - (Monday through Friday) as vacation.

Suggested Steps to build this project.
1. Set the project start date.
2. Adjust working hours and enter holidays for the project calendar.
3. Create your list of resources.
4. Enter the resource costs.
5. Adjust resource calendars.
6. Assign the printer to the 24-hour calendar and re-enter the printer's personal holidays.
7. Enter summary tasks.
8. Move the project tasks under the appropriate summary tasks.
9. Assign resources to each task.
10. Link your tasks.
11. Save into the C:/DATA/Project2016-1 folder.
12. Enter fixed costs for tasks and costs per use.
13. Look at the Project Statistics for Finish date and Costs.
14. Optimize. Look for tasks that could be done simultaneously, Make them Start-To-Start.

Insert Lead or Lag time.

15. Check for over-allocations and fix them.
16. Print the final Gantt Chart with the date range including extra days after project finish so it doesn't cut off tasks.
17. Review the *Reports Ribbon Tab* in Project 2013/2016 and the *Project Ribbon Tab→Reports* in Project 2010.

Index - Creating A Project

Work Weeks 24   **Zoom Slider** 4

www.ingramcontent.com/pod-product-compliance
Lightning Source LLC
Chambersburg PA
CBHW080605060326
40689CB00021B/4937